New to English

First Steps to Academic Success

Thomas Bye

McGraw-Hill

New to English, 1st Edition

Published by McGraw-Hill ESL/ELT, a business unit of The McGraw-Hill Companies, Inc., 1221 Avenue of the Americas, New York, NY 10020.

ISBN 978-0-07-319283-3
MHID 0-07-319283-X
3 4 5 6 7 8 9 QPD/QPD 12 11 10 09 08 07

Editorial director: Erik Gundersen
Developmental editor: Mari Vargo
Production manager: Juanita Thompson
Production coordinator: James D. Gwyn
Cover designer: Wee Design Group
Interior designer: Wee Design Group
Artists: Susan Detrich, Luigi Galante, Greg Harris, Judy Love, Don Morrison

McGraw-Hill

www.esl-elt.mcgraw-hill.com

The McGraw-Hill Companies

Acknowledgments

The authors and publisher would like to thank the following individuals who reviewed the *New to English* program at various stages of development and whose comments, reviews, and assistance were instrumental in helping us shape the project.

Carolyn Bohlman
Main East High School
Chicago, IL

Claire Bonskowski
Fairfax Public Schools
Fairfax, VA

Victoria Brioso
Broward County Public Schools
Ft. Lauderdale, FL

Karen Caddoo
Sheridan Public Schools
Sheridan, CO

Florence Decker
El Paso MS/HS
Franklin, TX

Trudy Freer-Alvarez
Houston Independent School District
Houston, TX

Leonor Guillen
Montgomery County Public Schools
Rockville, MD

Barbara Hernandez
Orange Unified School District
Orange, CA

Maryann Lyons
Francisco Middle School
San Francisco, CA

Susan Nordberg
Miami, FL

Jeanette Roy
Miami-Dade County Public Schools
Miami, FL

Steve Sloan
James Monroe High School
North Hills, CA

Leslie Eloise Somers
Miami-Dade County Public Schools
Miami, FL

Marie Stuart
San Gabriel Unified School District
San Gabriel, CA

Susan J. Watson
Horace Mann Middle School
San Francisco, CA

Thanks to the entire McGraw-Hill team for supporting the development of *New to English*. Special thanks to Mari Vargo for her ability to see both the forest and the trees, and to Erik Gundersen for promoting the *New to English* program.

About the Author

Thomas Bye is an educator and consultant in second language learning and teaching. He was a high school teacher and has served as coordinator of bilingual education as well as director of curriculum and strategic planning for a large school district. He has written other programs for English Learners. He holds a Ph.D. in linguistics from UCLA.

Dedication

New to English is dedicated to my family, David Bohne and Chipper.

Scope and Sequence

SECTION A: PHONICS AND SCHOOL VOCABULARY

Unit	Listening/ Oral Skills	Beginning Reading	Beginning Writing	Academic Learning	Phonics
1 I Know the Alphabet! page 4	Letters and words Following directions	Recognizing upper- and lowercase letters	Copying letters	The English alphabet Classroom actions	
2 I Know Numbers! page 6	Counting Following directions	Reading numbers	Printing numbers	Direction: right and left	
3 School Starts in September. page 8	Talking about things we like to do	Reading days and months by sight	Making a weekly calendar	Calendar Everyday activities	
4 Welcome to Kennedy High School! page 10	Expressing personal information	Reading personal information by sight	Writing personal information	School forms	
5 There's the Bell. page 12	Talking about things we do each day	Telling time	Making a daily schedule	Clock time Everyday activities	
6 How's It Going? page 16	Meeting and greeting others	Reading consonant sounds and letters *t* and *d*	Writing words that begin with *t* or *d* Writing a short sentence	Names	Consonants: *t, d*
7 This Is My Classroom. page 18	Following classroom directions	Reading consonant sounds and letters *p* and *b*	Writing words that begin with *p* or *b* Writing a short sentence	Classroom objects Classroom actions	Consonants: *b, p*
8 I Love Math! page 20	Expressing dimension: length, width, depth	Reading consonant sounds and letters *m* and *n*	Writing words that begin with *m* or *n*	Numbers and math Guessing and checking: measurement	Consonants: *m, n*

SECTION A: PHONICS AND SCHOOL VOCABULARY

Unit	Listening/ Oral Skills	Beginning Reading	Beginning Writing	Academic Learning	Phonics
9 This is My World! page 22	Expressing location Telling where you are from	Reading consonant sounds and letters *r* and *l*	Writing words that begin with *r* or *l* Writing a short sentence	Terms used in geography	Consonants: *l, r*
10 It's Time for P.E. page 24	Naming body parts Following action commands	Reading consonant sounds and letters *h* and *f*	Writing words that begin with *h* or *f* Writing a short sentence	Vocabulary used in P.E.: Sports verbs and objects	Consonants: *f, h*
11 English Class Is Fun! page 26	Following directions	Reading consonant sounds and letters *v* and *w*	Writing words that begin with *v* or *w* Writing a short sentence	Vocabulary used in English class: *nouns, verbs, sentences*, etc.	Consonants: *v, w*
12 Welcome to the Library! page 30	Expressing possession: *have*	Reading consonant sounds and letters *g, k, j,* and *y*	Writing words that begin with *g, k, j,* or *y* Writing a short sentence	Using the library	Consonants: *g, k, j, y*
13 I'm Hungry. Let's Have Lunch! page 32	Naming foods Ordering in a restaurant	Reading consonant sounds and letters *s* and *c*	Writing words that begin with *s* or *c* Writing a short sentence	School cafeteria language	Consonants: *c, s*
14 I'm an Artist. page 34	Naming colors and shapes Making and describing a collage	Reading consonant blends with *l* and *r*	Writing words that begin with blends Writing a short sentence	Vocabulary used in art class	Consonant blends
15 I Like Biology. page 36	Naming plants and animals Describing how animals move	Reading digraphs *ch, sh,* and *th*	Writing words that begin with digraphs	Vocabulary used in biology	Digraphs: *sh, ch, th*
16 School Is Out! page 40	Telling what you like to do for fun	Reading *s*-blends	Writing words that begin with s-blends Writing a short sentence	Recreational interests	*s*-blends

Scope and Sequence

SECTION B: BEGINNING TO READ

Unit	Listening/ Oral Skills	Target Sounds and Letters	Reading Skills	Writing Skills
1 I Have a Lot of Friends. page 42	Introductions Expressing possession: *have*	Short vowel /ă/ : *a* + consonant	Reading familiar words Sounding out new words Distinguishing final consonants Matching words to pictures Reading sentences for fluency Chanting for fluency	Writing sentences Making new words
2 My Room Is a Mess! page 46	Objects: *This is …* Describing objects	Short vowel /ĕ/: *e* + consonant		
3 I Feel Sick. page 50	Injury or illness Expressing temporary present: *Ed is singing.*	Short vowel /ĭ/: *i* + consonant		
4 Let's Have Fun! page 54	Things that are fun Expressing ability: *can*	Short vowels /ŏ/ and /ŭ/: *o* + consonant; *u* + consonant		
5 I Do It Every Day! page 58	Things you like to do Expressing habit	Long vowel /ā/: *a* + consonant + *e*; *ai* + consonant		
6 I See Animals. page 62	Naming and describing animals	Long vowel /ē/: *ee* + consonant; *ea* + consonant		
7 Everyone Likes Mike! page 66	Describing people and what they are doing	Long vowel /ī/: *i* + consonant + *e*; *ight*; *y*		
8 Let's Go to the Grocery Store. page 70	At the market Making requests	Long vowel /ō/, /ū/, /o͞o/: *o* + consonant (+ *e*); *oa* + consonant; *u* + consonant + *e*; *ew*; *oo*; *ui* + consonant		

SECTION C: INTEGRATING READING AND WRITING

Unit	Genres	Language Functions & Grammar	Academic Learning	Word Work & Phonics	Reading and Writing Skills
1 I Like Hip Hop! page 74	Venn diagram	Expressing preferences Subject pronouns	Comparing animals	Plurals (/s/ and /z/)	Reading labels and captions Reading connected sentences for meaning Developing fluency: timed reading tasks, dialogs, pair reading Writing labels and captions Writing connected sentences Using the writing process
2 This Is My Family Tree. page 84	Family tree	Asking and answering simple questions Possessive adjectives	Life science: using branching diagrams to classify	Sounding out words with the letters *ou*: *out, rough*	
3 This Is My Life. page 94	Personal timeline	Expressing habitual actions Parts of speech: nouns, verbs, and adjectives	History: using timelines to show sequence	Sounding out words with the letters *ow*: *snow, town*	
4 I Can Do Things. page 104	Flow diagram	Giving how-to instructions Affirmative present tense statements	Life science: flow diagrams to show the life cycle	Long plurals; irregular plurals	
5 Let's Find Out. page 114	Column graph	Expressing preferences Negative present tense statements	Using column graphs to present numerical data	The schwa /ə/ sound in unstressed syllables	
6 Big, Tall, and Wide page 124	Scale diagram	Describing objects and animals Present tense of *be* + adjectives	Science: using scale diagrams to compare	*r*-controlled vowels	

To the Student

Welcome to *New to English*! This book is written just for you. *New to English* will help you learn English.

You will learn English sounds and letters. You will also learn words you can use at school.

You will learn to read and write words.

You will learn to read and write sentences.

Best of all, you will get to work with others—talking, thinking, and doing and making things as you learn English together.

This is going to be a great year. Have fun!

To the Teacher

Welcome to *New to English*—an entry-level reading and writing program that builds foundations for reading fluency and prepares students for *On Location*, Books 1–3.

New to English offers a research-based approach that honors the findings of the *National Reading Panel* that support the direct teaching of phonemic awareness and phonics while promoting instructional practices that develop language and literacy through focus on comprehension. *New to English* recognizes that learning to read and write is developmental and that students must first learn to hear and produce the sounds of English before they read and write. The program also recognizes that beginning readers develop fluency in predictable stages as they learn how an alphabetic language like English works.

BUILDING FOUNDATIONS FOR READING FLUENCY

New to English is organized in three developmental sections to accommodate the differing needs of newcomer students—

- Students at the pre-alphabetic stage—that is, those who do not yet understand that there is a systematic relationship between the sounds and letters of English—begin with Section A where they learn the alphabet and numbers, how to tell time and read the calendar, and how to read simple schedules. They learn to distinguish sounds and identify sound/letter correspondences. They develop beginning writing skills and they learn basic vocabulary they will need in their content-area classes.
- Students at the partial alphabetic stage—those who have learned many sound/letter relationships and are ready to tackle simple words—begin with Section B where they learn to manipulate sounds and to blend sounds to decode short words. They continue to build academic vocabulary.
- Students at the fully alphabetic stage—those who have the decoding skills needed to tackle unfamiliar words and short sentences—begin with Section C where they fine-tune phonics skills, begin to read and write in the content areas, and learn basic English grammar.

The audio program includes activities that help students hear the sounds and words of English. Each reading selection in the Student Book is included, providing authentic models of language use. An audio script is provided at the back of the book for teachers who choose not to use audio players in class.

A wrap-around **Teacher's Edition** provides step-by-step guidance through every lesson, helping the teacher use best teaching practices to develop beginning reading and writing skills.

The **Assessment System** includes a diagnostic test to help the teacher place the student, end-of-section assessments, and an end-of-level test.

Welcome to New to English!

In Section A: Phonics and School Vocabulary, students...

learn **sound/letter relationships** in context.

develop **phonemic awareness.**

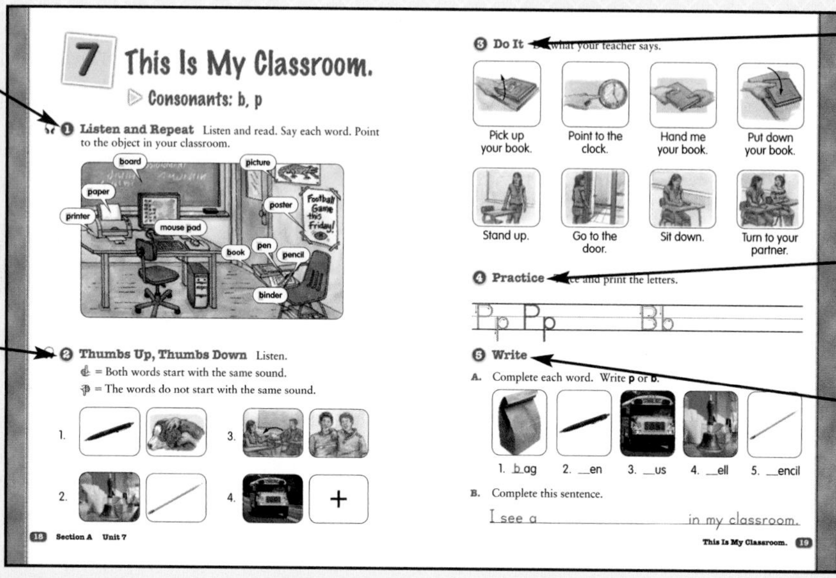

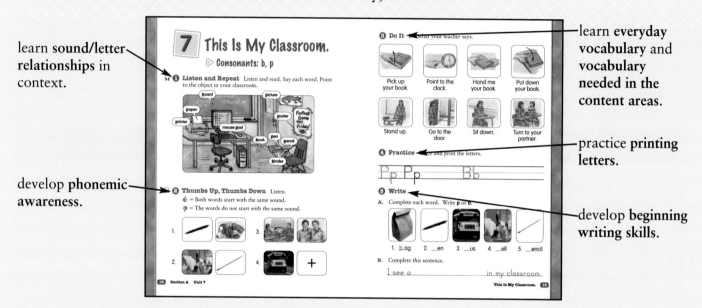

learn **everyday vocabulary** and **vocabulary needed in the content areas.**

practice **printing letters.**

develop **beginning writing skills.**

7 This Is My Classroom.
Consonants: b, p
1 Listen and Repeat Listen and read. Say each word. Point to the object in your classroom.
board
picture
paper
printer
poster
mouse pad
Football Game this Friday!
book
pen
pencil
binder
2 Thumbs Up, Thumbs Down Listen.
= Both words start with the same sound.
= The words do not start with the same sound.
1.
2.
3.
4.
3 Do It
Pick up your book.
Point to the clock.
Hand me your book.
Put down your book.
Stand up.
Go to the door.
Sit down.
Turn to your partner.
4 Practice
Pp Pp Bb
5 Write
A. Complete each word. Write p or b.
1. bag 2. __en 3. __us 4. __ell 5. __encil
B. Complete this sentence.
I see a in my classroom.
18 Section A Unit 7
This Is My Classroom. 19

In Section B: Beginning to Read, students...

identify sound/ letter patterns in words and **learn common words in context.**

practice **sounding out words**-as they develop **new vocabulary.**

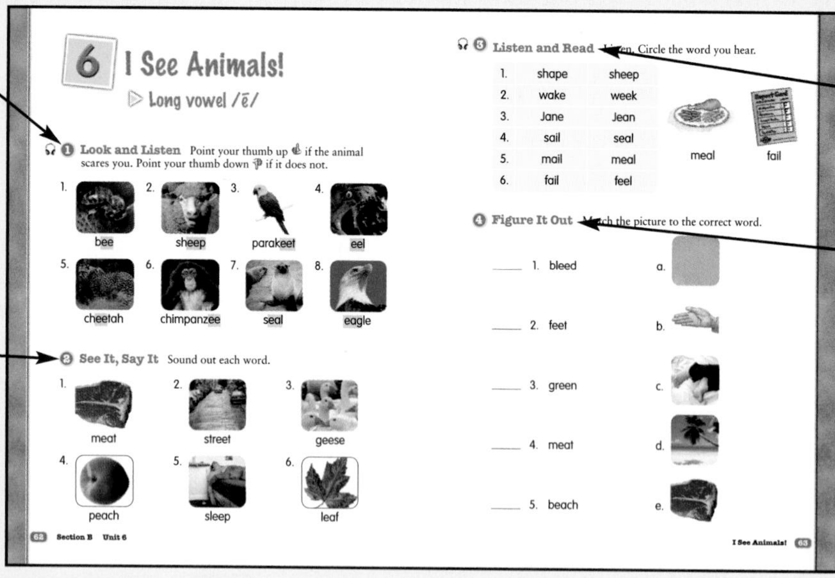

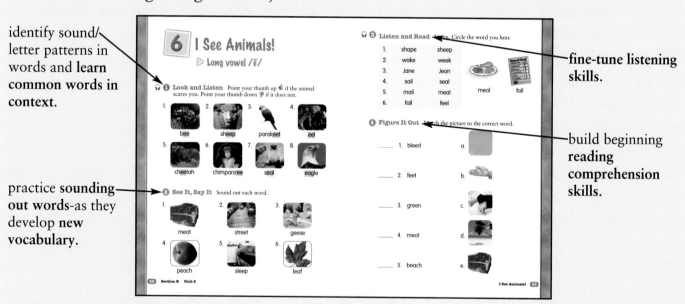

fine-tune listening skills.

build beginning **reading comprehension skills.**

Later in the unit, students practice **reading simple sentences**, work with vocabulary words, and practice **stress, rhythm, and intonation in a short chant.**

In Section C: Integrating Reading and Writing, students...

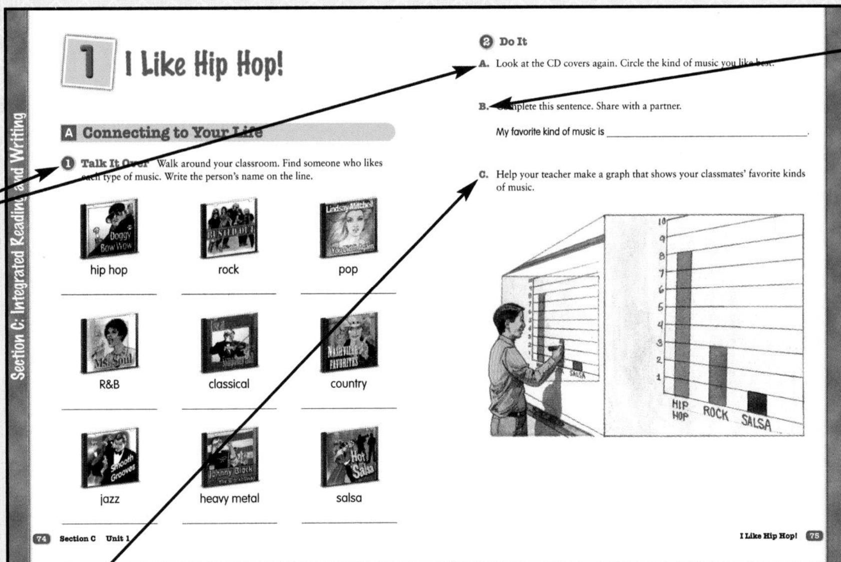

Section C: Integrated Reading and Writing

1 I Like Hip Hop!

A Connecting to Your Life

1 Talk It Over Walk around your classroom. Find someone who likes each type of music. Write the person's name on the line.

hip hop ______ rock ______ pop ______

R&B ______ classical ______ country ______

jazz ______ heavy metal ______ salsa ______

2 Do It

A. Look at the CD covers again. Circle the kind of music you like best.

B. Complete this sentence. Share with a partner.

My favorite kind of music is ______________________.

C. Help your teacher make a graph that shows your classmates' favorite kinds of music.

74 Section C Unit 1 — I Like Hip Hop! 75

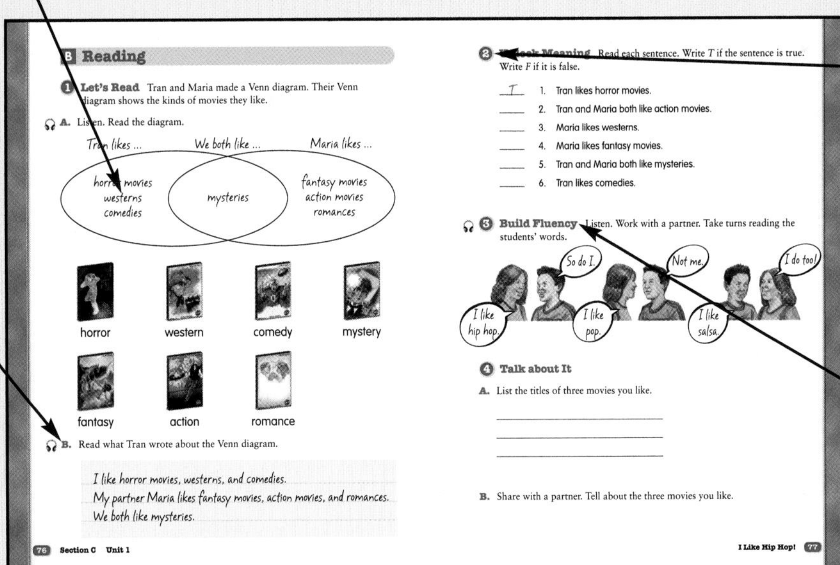

B Reading

1 Let's Read Tran and Maria made a Venn diagram. Their Venn diagram shows the kinds of movies they like.

A. Listen. Read the diagram.

horror western comedy mystery

fantasy action romance

B. Read what Tran wrote about the Venn diagram.

I like horror movies, westerns, and comedies.
My partner Maria likes fantasy movies, action movies, and romances.
We both like mysteries.

2 Check Meaning Read each sentence. Write *T* if the sentence is true. Write *F* if it is false.

T 1. Tran likes horror movies.
____ 2. Tran and Maria both like action movies.
____ 3. Maria likes westerns.
____ 4. Maria likes fantasy movies.
____ 5. Tran and Maria both like mysteries.
____ 6. Tran likes comedies.

3 Build Fluency Listen. Work with a partner. Take turns reading the students' words.

4 Talk about It

A. List the titles of three movies you like.

____

____

____

B. Share with a partner. Tell about the three movies you like.

76 Section C Unit 1 — I Like Hip Hop! 77

learn to talk about themselves and their personal preferences in **brief exchanges with classmates.**

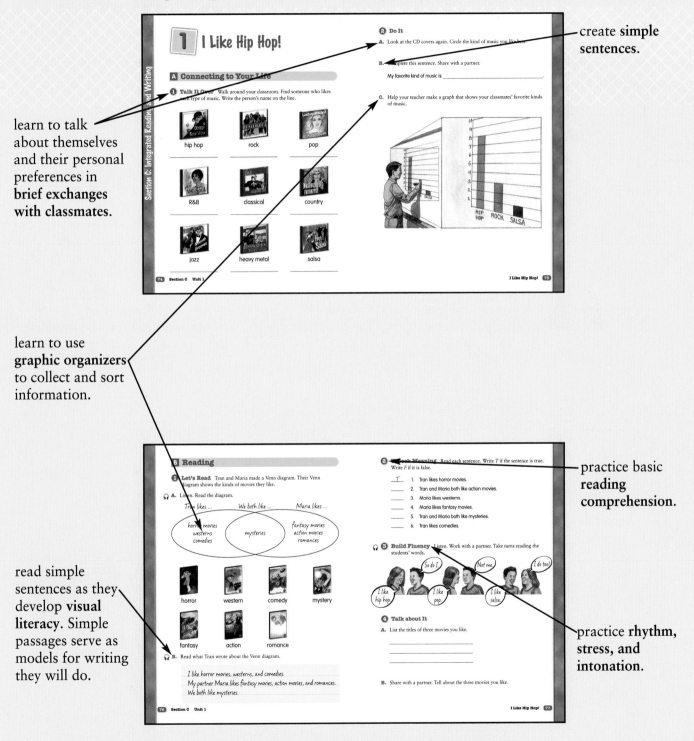

create **simple sentences.**

learn to use **graphic organizers** to collect and sort information.

practice basic **reading comprehension.**

read simple sentences as they develop **visual literacy.** Simple passages serve as models for writing they will do.

practice **rhythm, stress, and intonation.**

Later in the unit, students continue to build **phonics and decoding skills** and practice **listening and speaking.** They also learn and practice a **basic grammar point,** learn additional **content-area vocabulary,** and produce **simple written products.**

Welcome to School!

▷ Section A, Units 1–5

Listen and Repeat

4. students
3. girl
5. notebook

1 I Know the Alphabet!

Letters

1 Listen and Repeat

A. Listen. Say each letter.

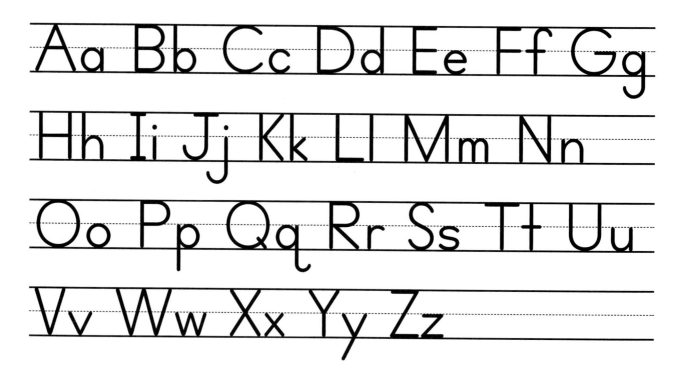

Aa Bb Cc Dd Ee Ff Gg

Hh Ii Jj Kk Ll Mm Nn

Oo Pp Qq Rr Ss Tt Uu

Vv Ww Xx Yy Zz

B. Listen. Repeat.

2 Do It Do what your teacher says.

Make lines.

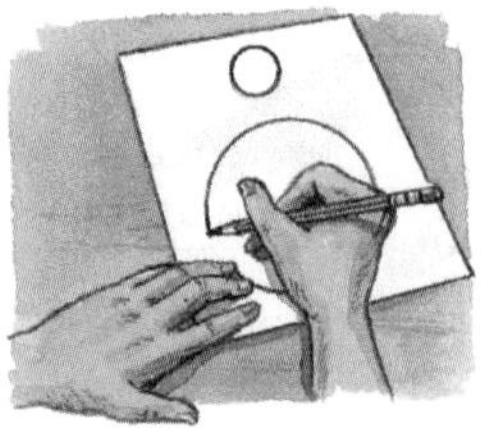

Make circles.

Make curves.

3 **Practice** Trace the letters.

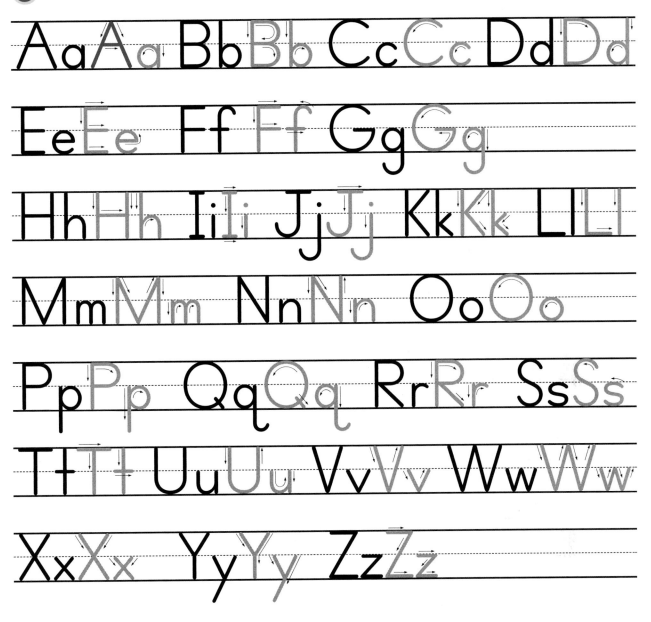

Aa Aa Bb Bb Cc Cc Dd Dd

Ee Ee Ff Ff Gg Gg

Hh Hh Ii Ii Jj Jj Kk Kk Ll Ll

Mm Mm Nn Nn Oo Oo

Pp Pp Qq Qq Rr Rr Ss Ss

Tt Tt Uu Uu Vv Vv Ww Ww

Xx Xx Yy Yy Zz Zz

4 **Write** Copy each word.

1. 

ask

a

2. 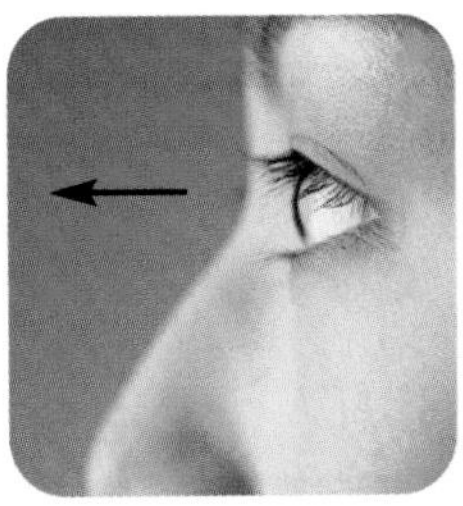

see

3. 

read

4. 

listen

2 I Know Numbers!

Numbers

1 Listen and Repeat Listen and read. Say each number.

1 one	2 two	3 three	4 four	5 five
6 six	7 seven	8 eight	9 nine	10 ten

11 eleven	12 twelve	13 thirteen	14 fourteen	15 fifteen
16 sixteen	17 seventeen	18 eighteen	19 nineteen	20 twenty
21 twenty-one	22 twenty-two	23 twenty-three	24 twenty-four	25 twenty-five
26 twenty-six	27 twenty-seven	28 twenty-eight	29 twenty-nine	30 thirty
40 forty	50 fifty	60 sixty	70 seventy	80 eighty
90 ninety	100 one hundred	101 one hundred one	102 one hundred two	200 two hundred

2 Thumbs Up, Thumbs Down Listen.

- 👍 = matches the number
- 👎 = does not match the number

a. 4 b. 9 c. 14 d. 31 e. 85

3 Do It Open the locks. Circle the numbers.

1. 

Turn right to five.

2. 

Turn left to twenty.

3. 

Turn right to thirty.

4. 

Turn right to ten.

5. 

Turn left to fifteen.

6. 

Turn right to twenty-five.

4 Practice Trace and print the numbers.

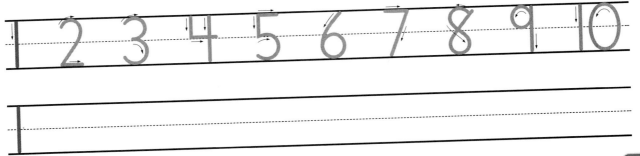

1 2 3 4 5 6 7 8 9 10

3 School Starts in September.

Days, months, and dates

1 Listen and Repeat

A. Listen and read. Say each day.

September

Sunday	Monday	Tuesday	Wednesday	Thursday	Friday	Saturday
		1	2	3	4	5
6	7	8	9	10	11	12
13	14	15	16	17	18	19
20	21	22	23	24	25	26
27	28	29	30			

1. January
2. February
3. March
4. April
5. May
6. June
7. July
8. August
9. September
10. October
11. November
12. December

B. Look at the calendar. Listen. Say the dates.

C. Listen. Say the months.

2 Thumbs Up, Thumbs Down

Listen to each date.

(thumbs up) = matches the date

(thumbs down) = does not match the date

1. September 6
2. December 13
3. May 20
4. October 10
5. February 14
6. August 30

3 **Do It** What do you like to do? Act it out. Watch and guess.

dance

draw

talk on the phone

play baseball

go to a movie

work on the computer

read a book

4 **Write** Make a calendar. Add the days and dates. Write something you want to do for each day.

Monday May 5	______ ______	Wednesday ______	Thursday ______	______ ______
play baseball				

4 Welcome to Kennedy High School!

▷ Personal information

1 Listen and Repeat Listen and read. Repeat Pablo's words.

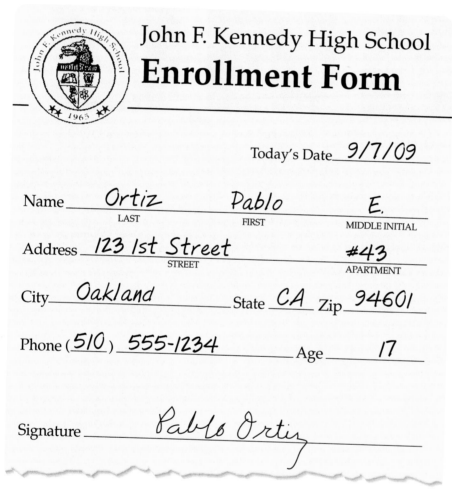

John F. Kennedy High School

Enrollment Form

Today's Date 9/7/09

Name Ortiz (LAST) Pablo (FIRST) E. (MIDDLE INITIAL)

Address 123 1st Street (STREET) #43 (APARTMENT)

City Oakland State CA Zip 94601

Phone (510) 555-1234 Age 17

Signature Pablo Ortiz

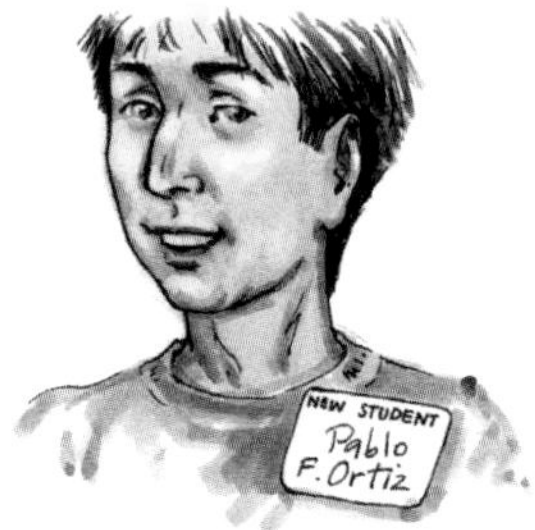

name

signature

2 Thumbs Up, Thumbs Down Listen to the sentences. Are they true or false?

👍 = true

👎 = false

❸ **Do It** Do what your teacher says.

1.

Say your name.

2.

Spell your first name.

3.

Say your phone number.

4.

Tell how old you are.

❹ **Write** Fill out this form. Please print. Sign your name.

Today's Date ______________

Name ____
LAST FIRST MIDDLE INITIAL

Address ____
STREET APARTMENT

City ______________________ State ______ Zip __________

Phone (_____) ______________________ Age __________

Signature ____

5 There's the Bell!

1 Listen and Repeat Listen and read. Say each time.

Morning (a.m.)

8:00
It is eight o'clock.

9:15
It is nine fifteen.

10:30
It is ten thirty.

11:45
It is eleven forty-five.

Afternoon (p.m.)

12:00
It is twelve o'clock.
It is noon.

1:20
It is one twenty.

2:40
It is two forty.

3:10
It is three ten.

2 Thumbs Up, Thumbs Down Listen.

👍 = matches the time you see

👎 = does not match the time you see

1. 2:10
2. 6:30
3. 8:15
4. 9:20
5. 10:40
6. 12:00
7. 1:35
8. 2:00

3 Do It What do you do in the evening or at night? Act it out. Watch and guess.

eat dinner

read a magazine

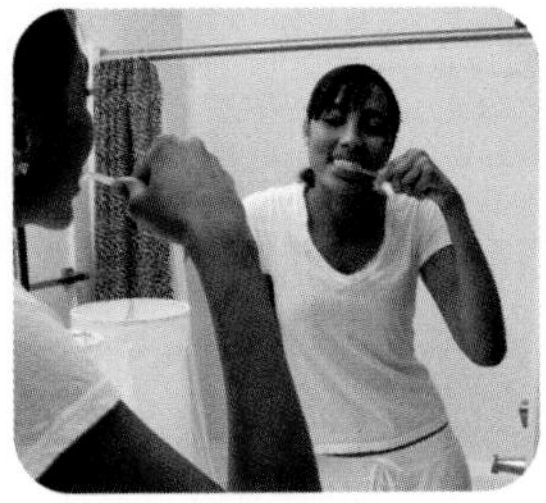

brush your teeth

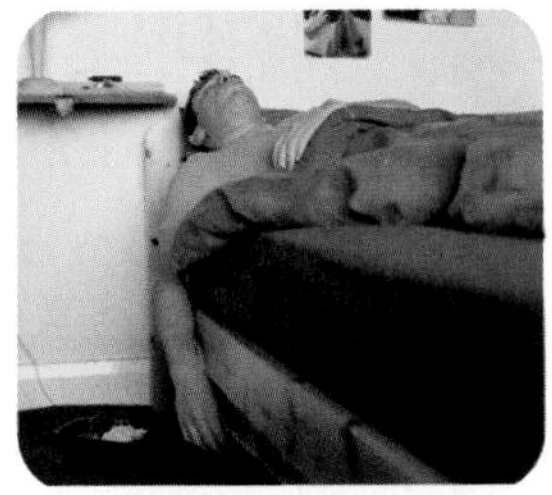

go to bed/ sleep

4 Practice Write the times.

1. 
2. 
3. 
4. 

8:

5 Write Make your own schedule. Write the times.

I wake up.

School begins.

I eat lunch.

School ends.

1. I wake up. 6:00
2. School begins. ________
3. I eat lunch. ________
4. School ends. ________
5. I eat dinner. ________
6. I go to bed. ________

My Morning Classes

▶ Section A, Units 6-11

Listen and Repeat

2. P.E.
3. add
4. subtract
5. multiply
6. divide

6 How's It Going?

Consonants: d, t

1 Listen and Repeat
Listen to each student. Introduce yourself.

2 Thumbs Up, Thumbs Down
Listen.

👍 = Both words start with the same sound.

👎 = The words do not start with the same sound.

1.  

2.  

3. 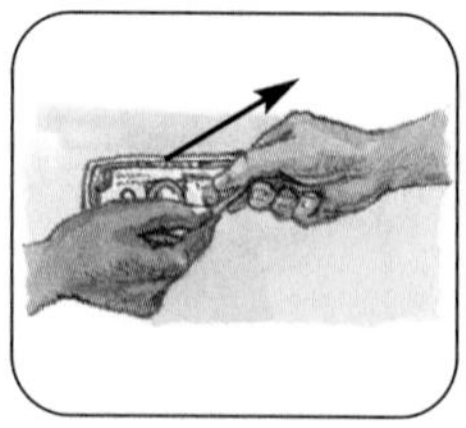 

4.  

3 Do It Meet and greet your classmates.

4 Practice Trace and print the letters.

Tt Tt

Dd

5 Write

A. Complete each word. Write **t** or **d**.

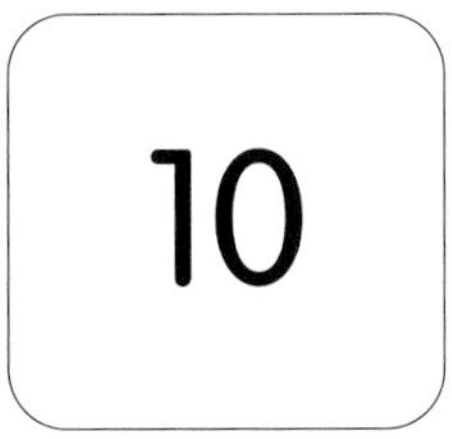

1. d og
2. __en
3. __ance
4. __raw
5. __alk

B. Complete this sentence.

My name is ______________________________.

7 This Is My Classroom.

▷ Consonants: b, p

1 Listen and Repeat Listen and read. Say each word. Point to the object in your classroom.

2 Thumbs Up, Thumbs Down Listen.

👍 = Both words start with the same sound.

👎 = The words do not start with the same sound.

1.  

3.  

2.  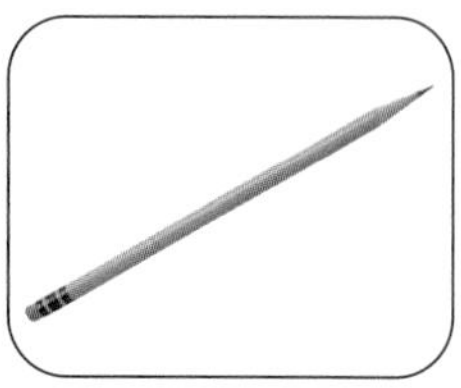

4. 

3 Do It Do what your teacher says.

Pick up your book.

Point to the clock.

Hand me your book.

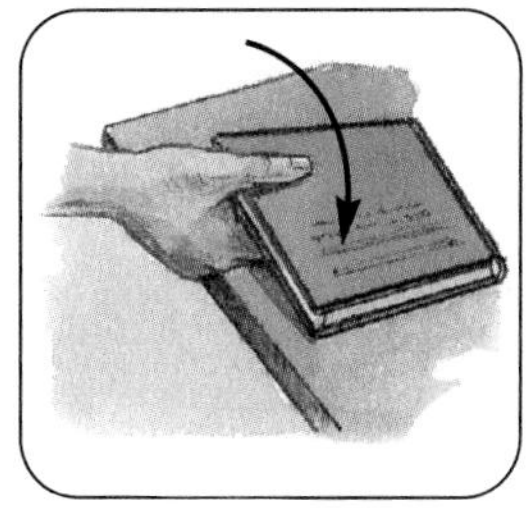
Put down your book.

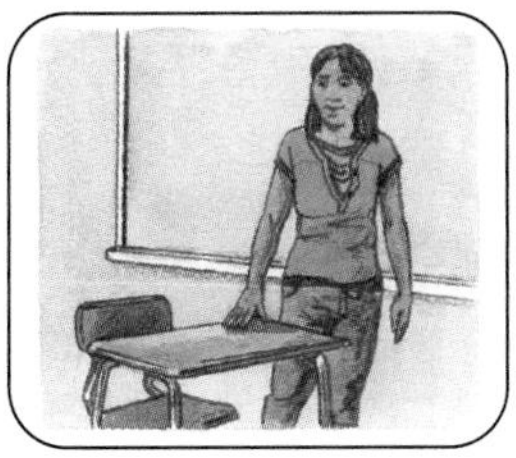
Stand up.

Go to the door.

Sit down.

Turn to your partner.

4 Practice Trace and print the letters.

Pp Pp Bb

5 Write

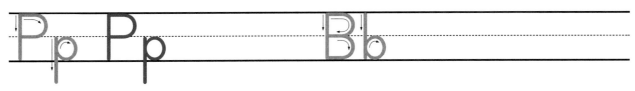

A. Complete each word. Write **p** or **b**.

1. b ag

2. __en

3. __us

4. __ell

5. __encil

B. Complete this sentence.

I see a ____________________ in my classroom.

8 I Love Math!

Consonants: m, n

1 Listen and Repeat

Listen and read. Say each sentence.

5+4= 9
Let's add numbers. Five plus four equals nine.

14-5 = 9
Let's subtract. Fourteen minus five equals nine.

3×3= 9
Let's multiply. Three times three equals nine.

90÷10= 9
Let's divide. Ninety divided by ten equals nine.

2 Thumbs Up, Thumbs Down

Listen.

= Both words start with the same sound.

= The words do not start with the same sound.

1.  

2.  

3. $2 + 2 = 4$ 

4.  

❸ Do It Guess and check.

A. Make a guess.

a marker

a notebook

a magazine rack

B. Check your guess. Use a ruler or tape measure.

❹ Practice Trace and print the letters.

Mm Mm Nn

❺ Write

Complete each word. Write **m** or **n**.

1. m̲an

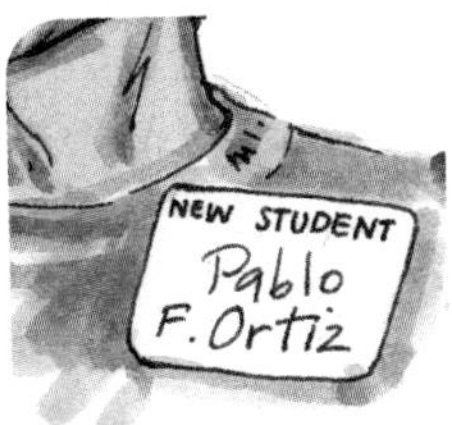

2. __ame

3. __oon

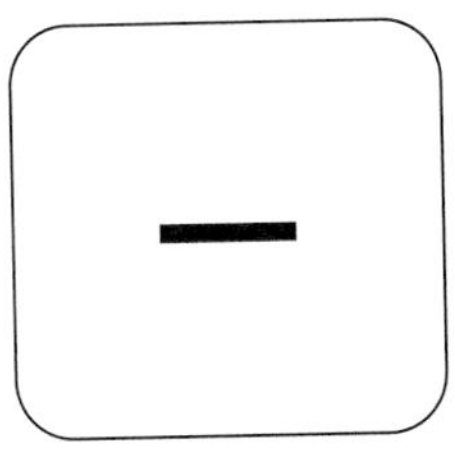

4. __inus

5. __ight

9 This Is My World!

▷ Consonants: l, r

1 Listen and Repeat Listen and read. Say each word or sentence. Point to the places.

I live in a city. I live in San Francisco.

My city is in a state. I live in California.

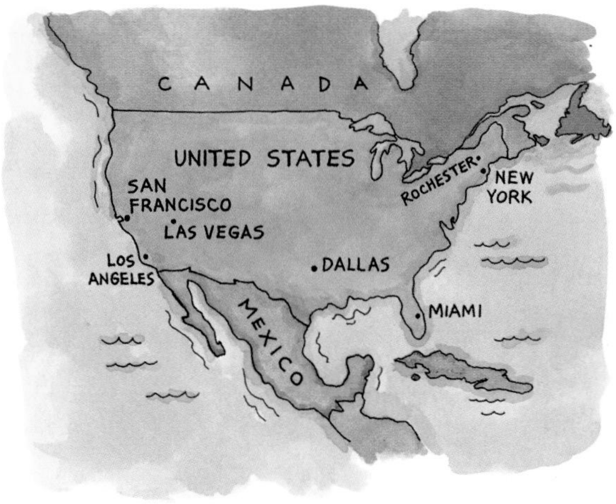

My state is in a country. I live in the United States.

I live on planet Earth.

2 Do It Say where you are from.

I'm from Laos.

I come from Latvia.

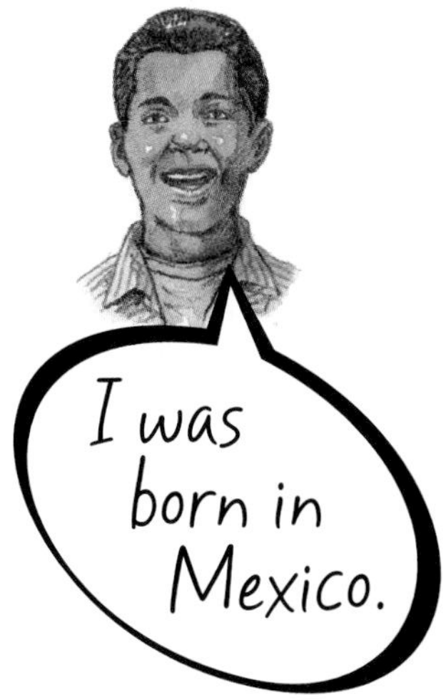

I was born in Mexico.

3 Practice Trace and print the letters.

Ll Ll Rr

4 Write

A. Complete each word. Write **l** or **r**.

1. r uler 2. __unch 3. __ead 4. __ocker 5. __isten

B. Complete this sentence.

My family comes from ____________________.

10 It's Time for P.E.

Consonants: f, h

1 Listen and Repeat Listen and read. Say each word. Then follow the commands.

② Do It Listen to your teacher. Act it out.

throw far

catch

pitch

hit

walk

jog

run fast

jump high

③ Practice Trace and print the letters.

Ff Ff Hh

④ Write

A. Complete each word. Write **f** or **h**.

1. h it

2. __and

½
3. __alf

5
4. __ive

5. jump __igh

B. Complete this sentence.

I like P.E. I like to ______________________.

11 English Class Is Fun!

▷ Consonants: v, w

1 Listen and Repeat Listen and read.

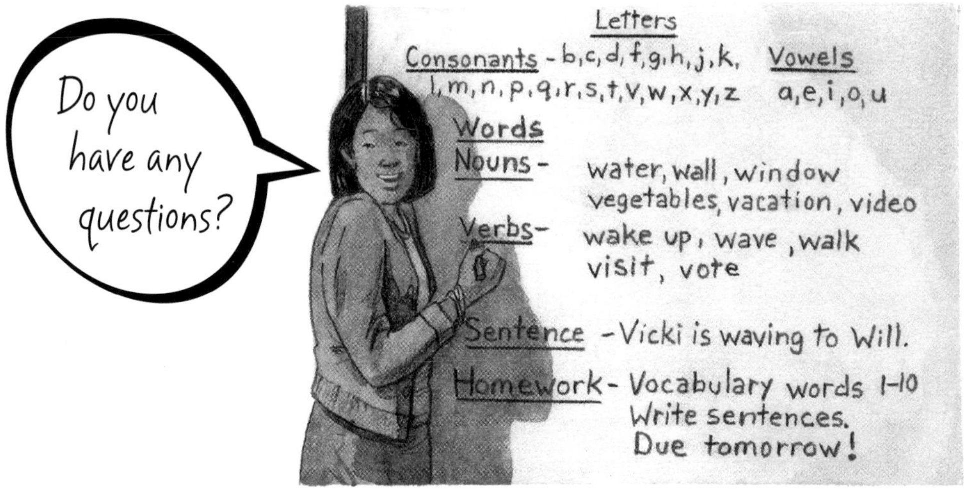

Do you have any questions?
Letters
Consonants - b, c, d, f, g, h, j, k, l, m, n, p, q, r, s, t, v, w, x, y, z
Vowels a, e, i, o, u
Words
Nouns - water, wall, window vegetables, vacation, video
Verbs - wake up, wave, walk visit, vote
Sentence - Vicki is waving to Will.
Homework - Vocabulary words 1-10 Write sentences. Due tomorrow!

2 Thumbs Up, Thumbs Down Listen.

👍 = Both words start with the same sound.

👎 = The words do not start with the same sound.

1.  

2. 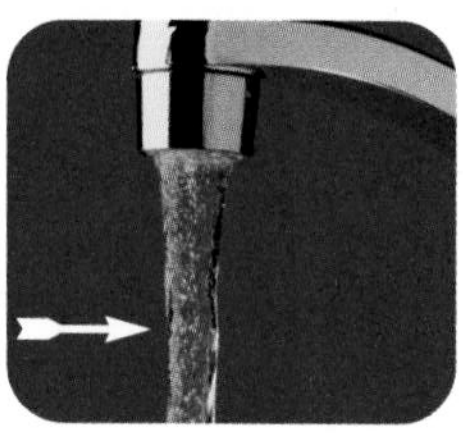 

3.  

4.  

3 Do It Listen. Do what you hear.

circle

underline

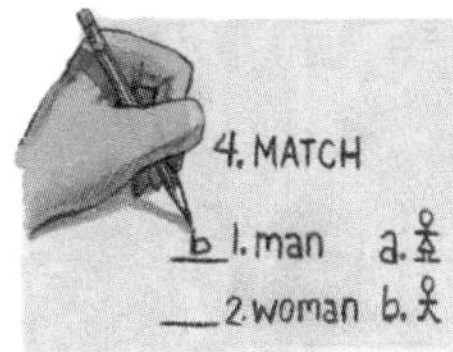

match

1. Circle.
   a. v
   b. w
2. Underline.
   a. v
   b. w
3. Match.
   ___ 1. volcano
   ___ 2. window

a. 

b. 

4 Practice Trace and print the letters.

Vv Vv Ww

5 Write

A. Complete each word. Write **v** or **w**.

1. v egetable 2. __eek 3. __oman 4. __alk 5. __ase

B. Complete this sentence.

My homework tonight is ______________________.

My Afternoon at School

▷ Section A, Units 12–15

Listen and Repeat

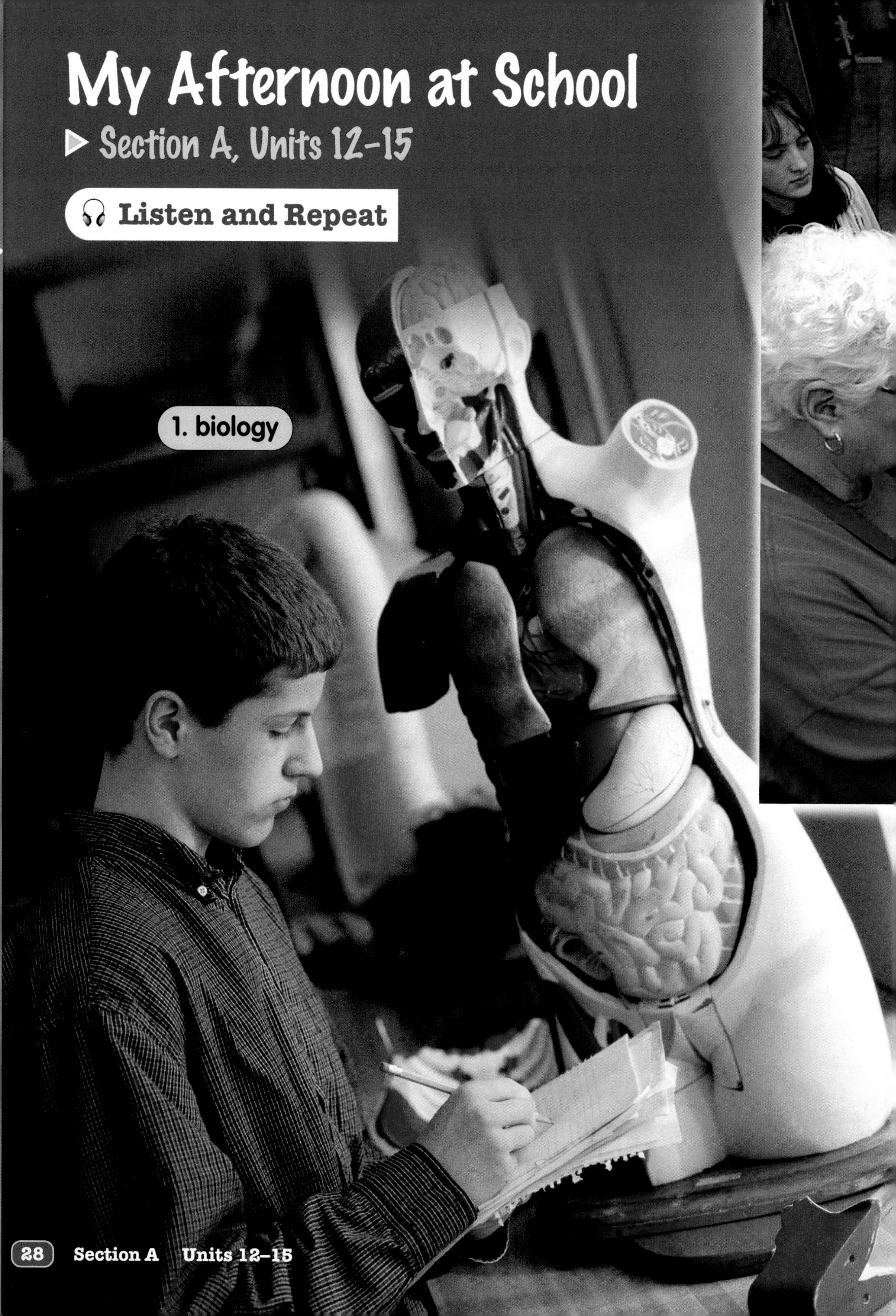

1. biology

Section A: Phonics and School Vocabulary

2. cafeteria
3. library
4. librarian

12 Welcome to the Library.

▷ Consonants: g, k, j, y

❶ Listen and Repeat Listen. Read the titles.

❷ Thumbs Up, Thumbs Down Listen.

👍 = Both words start with the same sound.

👎 = The words do not start with the same sound.

1.  

2.  

3.  

4. 

3 Do It Work in a group. Match the pictures to the words. Write the letters on the lines.

__e__ 1. newspaper

_____ 2. book

_____ 3. magazine

_____ 4. dictionary

_____ 5. encyclopedias

a.

b.

c.

d.

e.

4 Practice Print the letters.

Gg Gg Jj

Kk Yy

5 Write

A. Complete each word. Write **g**, **j**, **k**, or **y**.

1. _k_ing

2008
2. __ear

3. __ump

4. __ame

5. __og

B. Complete this sentence.

I like to read books about ____.

13 I'm Hungry. Let's Have Lunch!

Consonants: c, s

1 Listen and Repeat Listen. Say each food and drink.

❷ Do It Practice ordering in a restaurant. Act it out.

❸ Practice Trace and print the letters.

Cc Cc Ss

❹ Write

A. Complete each word. Write **c** or **s**.

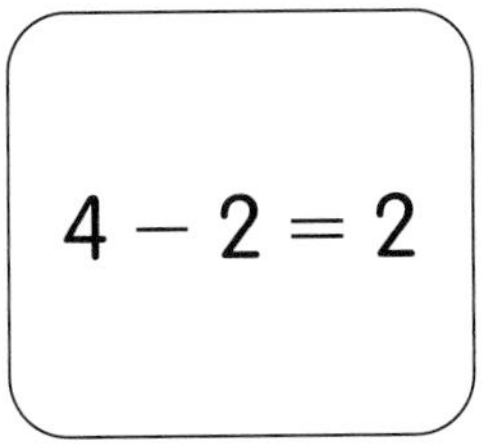

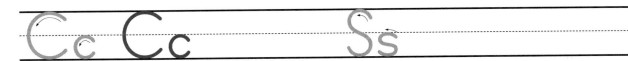

1. c alendar 2. __ubtract 3. __alad 4. __omputer

B. Complete this sentence.

My favorite food is ____________________.

14 I'm an Artist.

Consonant blends

1 Listen and Repeat Listen. Say each color and shape.

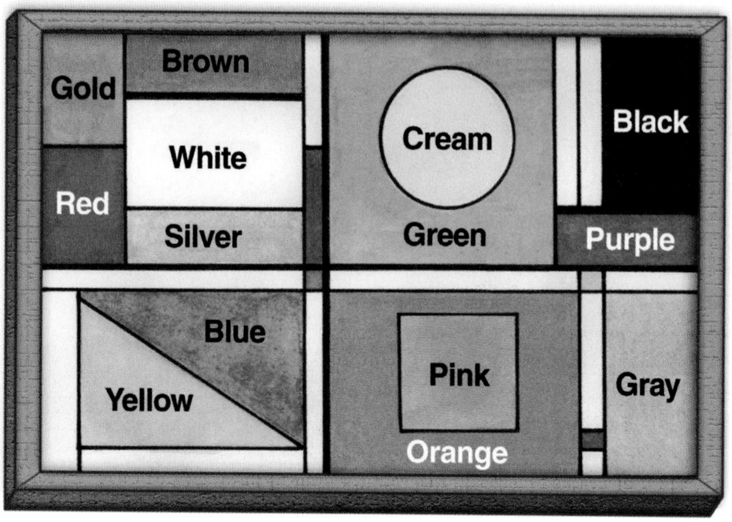

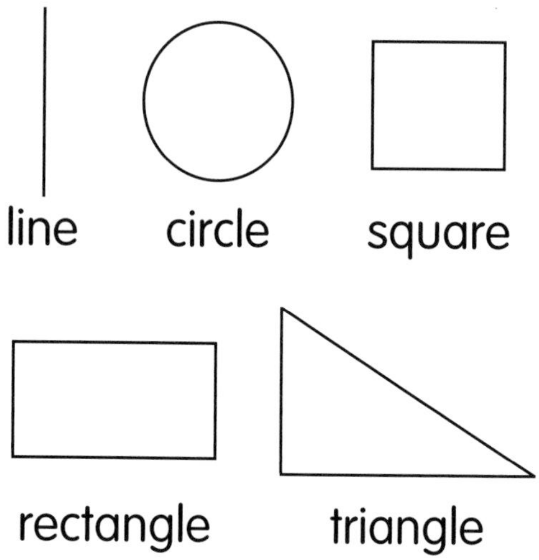

2 Thumbs Up, Thumbs Down Listen. Pay attention to the sounds of the first two letters of each word.

[Thumbs up] = Both words start with the same sounds.

[Thumbs down] = The words do not start with the same sounds.

1.  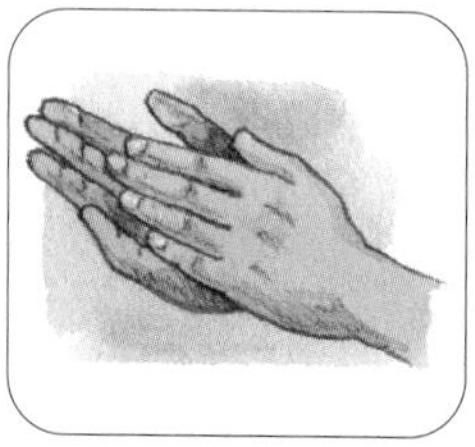

3.  

2. 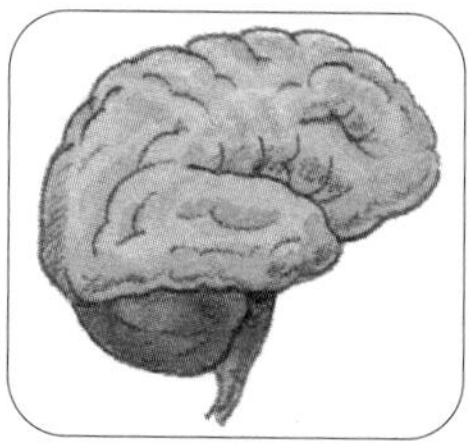 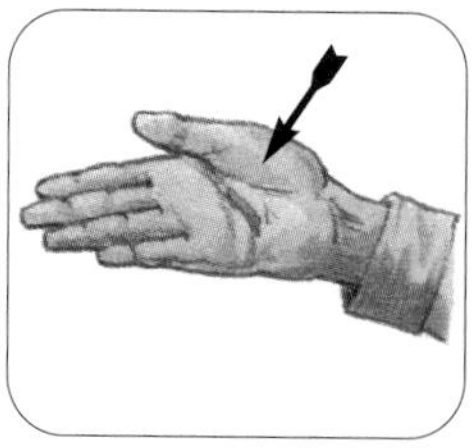

4. 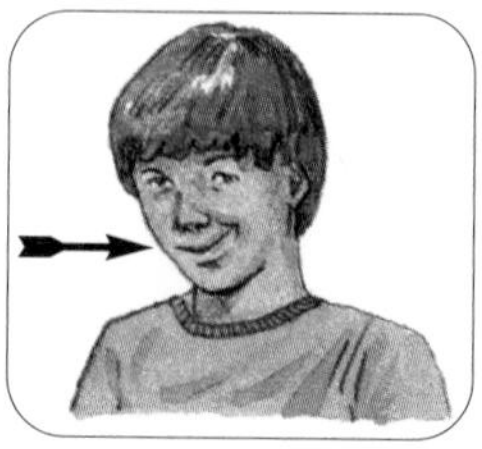 

3 Do It

A. Make a shape collage. Use paint and paper.

Use scissors.

Use paper.

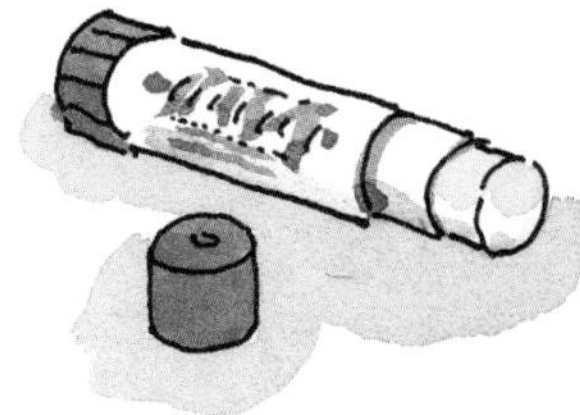

Use glue stick.

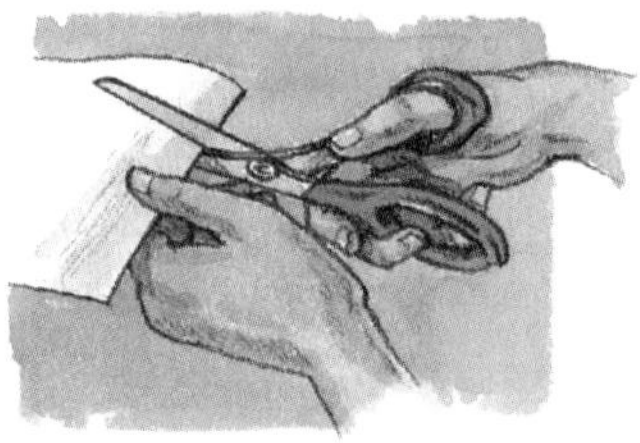

Cut.

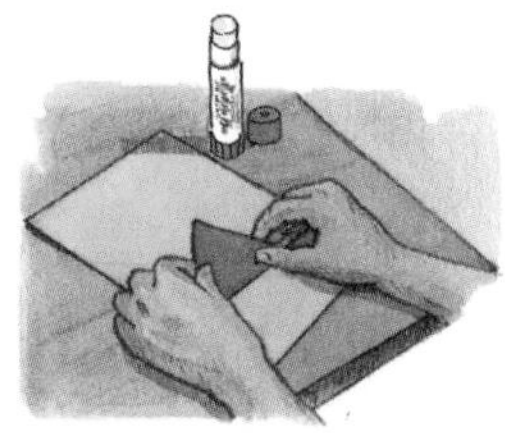

Glue.

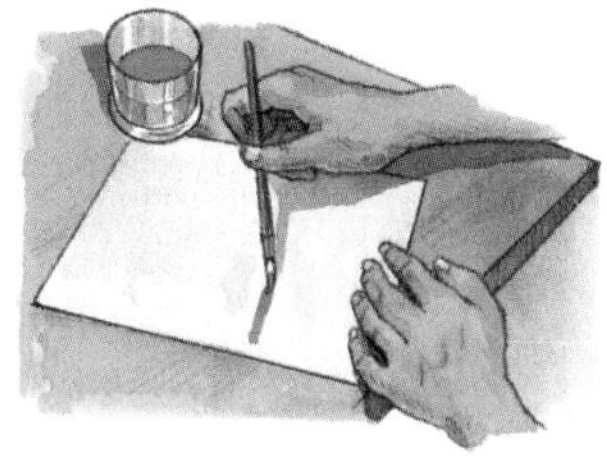

Paint.

B. Describe your collage. Name the shapes and colors.

4 Write

A. Complete each word. Use the letters below.

gl   cl   fl   br

1. br ush

2. ___ock

3. ___ag

4. ___obe

5. ___own

B. Complete this sentence. Use colors.

I have ____________ eyes and ____________ hair.

15 I Like Biology.

Digraphs: sh, ch, th

1 Listen and Repeat Listen. Say each plant or animal.

Plants

tree

flower

shrub or bush

grass

Animals

Fish

shark

shellfish

Birds

parrot

duck

Mammals

chimpanzee

panther

Insects

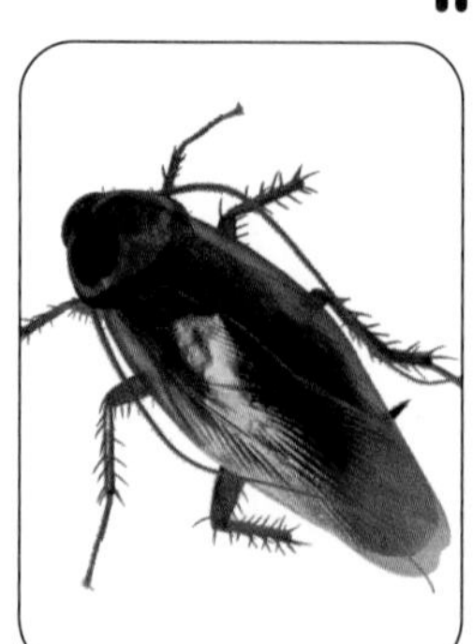
cockroach

bee

2 Do It

A. Look at the pictures. Learn how animals move.

fly

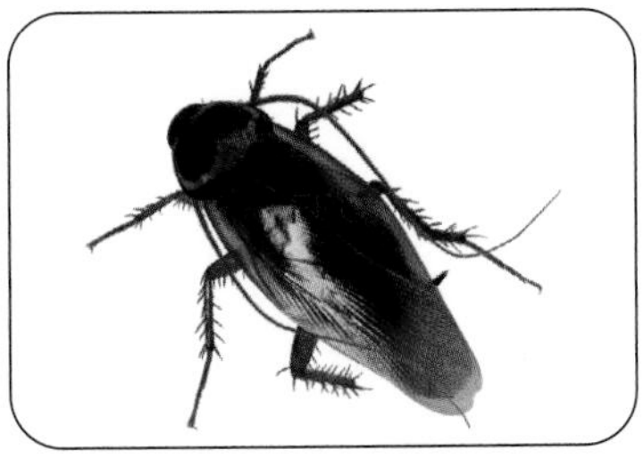

walk or crawl

swim

B. Work with a partner. How do animals move? Make sentences.

sheep

bees

sharks

rats

chipmunks

eagles

3 Write

Complete each word. Use **ch**, **sh**, or **th**.

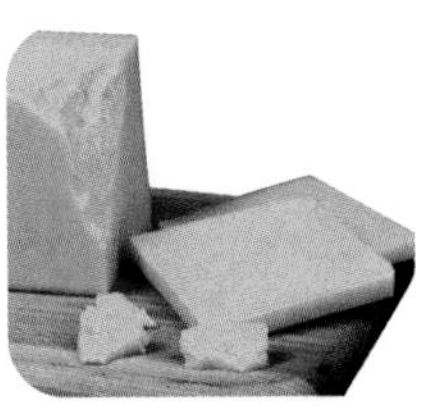

1. ___eese

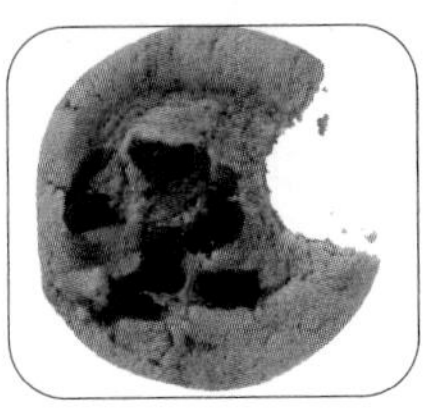

2. ___ocolate ___ip cookie

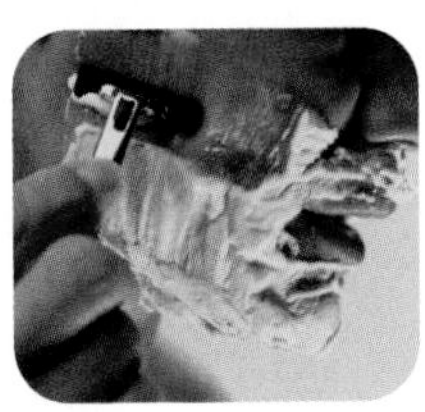

3. ___ave

4. ___umb

After School

▷ Section A, Unit 16

Listen and Repeat

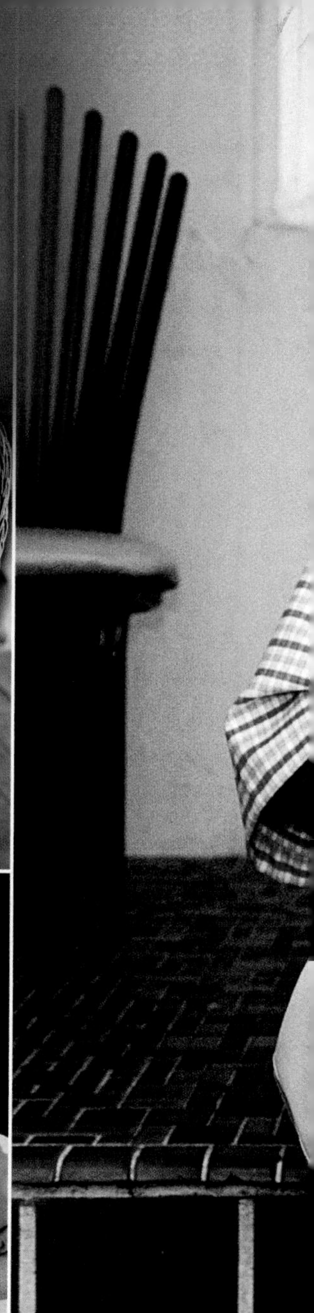

❸ Do It What do you do for thrills? Tell your classmates.

ski

snowboard

snorkel

scuba dive

sled

swim

❹ Write

A. Complete each word. Use the letters below.

sm sp st squ sw

1. __ep

2. __are

3. __ell

4. __im

5. __ell

B. Complete this sentence.

My favorite snack is ______________________________.

1 I Have a Lot of Friends!

Short vowel /ă/

1 Look and Listen
Listen and read along. Repeat.

1. 
I am Pam.

2. 
I am Tab.

3. 
I am Stan.

4. 
I am Ann.

5. 
I am Pat.

6. 
I am Frank.

7. 
I am Jack.

8. 
I am Chad.

2 See It, Say It
Sound out each name.

1. 
Hank

2. 
Zack

3. 
Nan

4. 
Sam

5. 
Jan

6. 
Brad

3 Listen and Read Listen. Circle the word you hear.

1.	rap	(rat)
2.	cat	cap
3.	man	map
4.	bad	bag
5.	pass	Pat
6.	jam	Jan

rap singer

4 Figure It Out Match the picture to the correct word.

__e__ 1. lab

_____ 2. snack

_____ 3. pan

_____ 4. dad

_____ 5. hand

a. 

b. 

c. 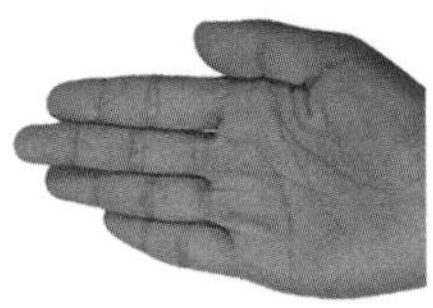

d. 

e. 

5 Shared Reading Help your teacher read each sentence.

1.

Jan has a fan.

2.

Pat has a cat.

3.

Dan has a map.

4.

Tab has a backpack.

5.

Fran has a black cat.

6.

Sam has a tan van.

6 Read and Write Look at the picture. Write the missing word.

rat	sad	cat	~~glad~~

1. Chad is glad.

2. Chad is ________.

3. Pat has a ________.

4. Tabby is catching a ________.

7 Make Words

A. Change the underlined letters in each word. Make new words. Use the letters below.

-at -ad -ap -ab -an -am -ack

1. c<u>ap</u> cat ______
2. m<u>an</u> ______
3. h<u>ad</u> ______
4. b<u>at</u> ______
5. s<u>ack</u> ______
6. p<u>an</u> ______

B. Share your words with your classmates.

8 Make Sentences

Choose one word from the unit. Write a sentence.

______.

9 Chant

Listen to the chant. Repeat.

Matt has a cat.
His cat is black.
His cat ate a rat.
What a good snack!

2 My Room Is a Mess!

▷ Short vowel /ĕ/

1 Look and Listen Listen and repeat. Point your thumb up if the word has a short /ĕ/ sound. Point your thumb down if the word has a short /ă/ sound.

2 See It, Say It Sound out each word.

1. 
Ed

2. 
test

3. 
check

4. 
men

5. 
wet

6. 

less

3 Listen and Read Listen. Circle the word you hear.

1.	bad	(bed)
2.	man	men
3.	pan	pen
4.	sand	send
5.	Pat	pet
6.	Tad	Ted

4 Figure It Out Match the picture to the correct word.

__a__ 1. nest

____ 2. bell

____ 3. spell

____ 4. ten

____ 5. check

____ 6. red

a. 

b. 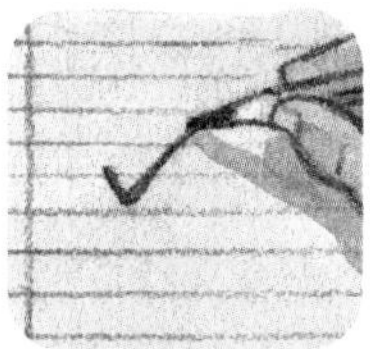

c. 

d. 

e. 

f. 10

5 Shared Reading Help your teacher read each sentence.

1. 

This is a shell.

2. 

This is a cell phone.

3. 

This is an egg.

4. 

This is a rat.
It is a pest.

5. 

This is a man.

6. 

These are two men.

6 Read and Write Look at the picture. Write the missing word.

bed	cell phone	~~mess~~	pet

1. My room is a ___mess___.

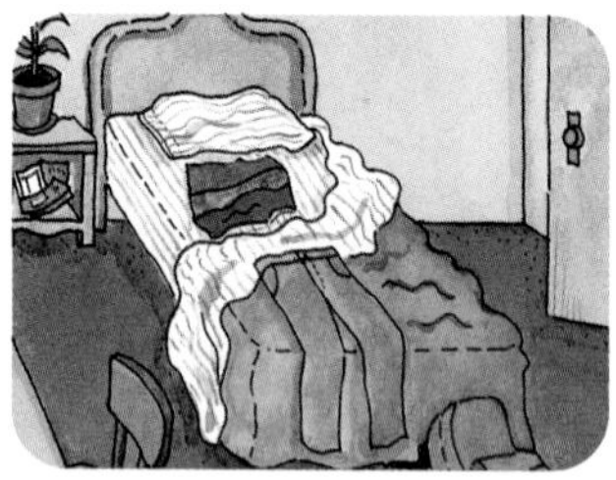

2. This is my ________.

3. This is my ________.

4. This is my ________.

7 Make Words

A. Change the underlined letters in each word. Make new words. Use the letters below.

-ed -et -en -ell -est -eck

1. b<u>at</u> bed ______
2. n<u>ap</u> ______
3. p<u>an</u> ______
4. t<u>ap</u> ______
5. ch<u>at</u> ______
6. r<u>at</u> ______

B. Share your words with your classmates.

8 Make Sentences

Choose one word from the unit. Write a sentence.

______.

9 Chant

Listen to the chant. Repeat.

Poor, poor Fred!
He fell off his sled
And he hit his head!
Now he's home in bed.

3 I Feel Sick.

▷ Short vowel /ĭ/

1 Look and listen Listen and read along. Repeat.

1.

My wrist hurts.

2.

I cut my finger.

3.

I twisted my ankle.

4.

I bit my lip.

5.

I hit my chin.

2 See It, Say It Sound out each word.

1.
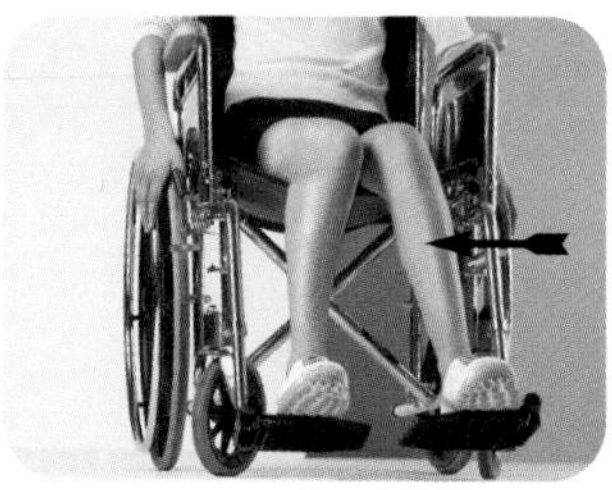
shin

2.
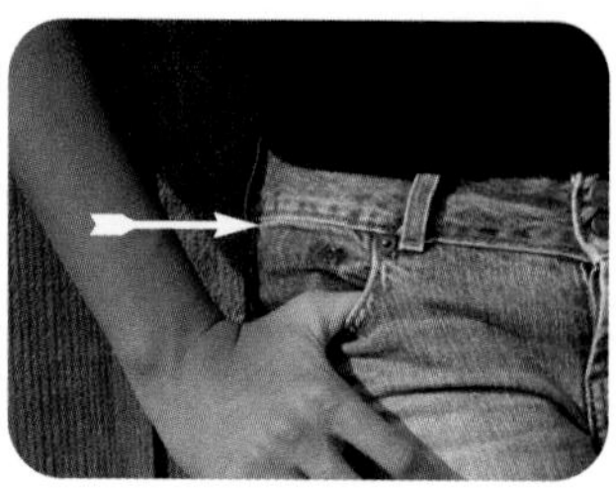
hip

3.

eyelid

3 Listen and Read Listen. Circle the word you hear.

1.	(thank)	think
2.	blank	blink
3.	hat	hit
4.	ten	tin
5.	pen	pin
6.	spell	spill

blink

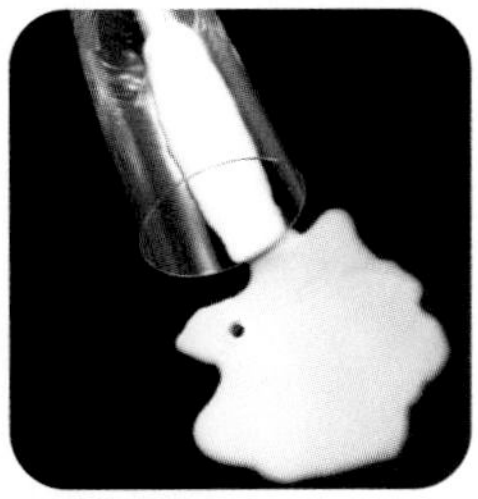
spill

4 Figure It Out Match the picture to the correct word.

d 1. stink — a. 

_____ 2. pink — b. 

_____ 3. sit down — c. 

_____ 4. grin — d. 

_____ 5. pick up — e. 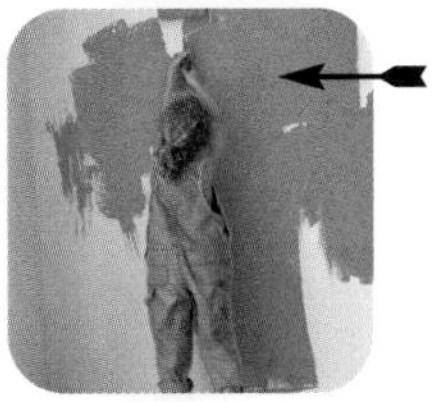

_____ 6. sing — f. 

5 Shared Reading Help your teacher read each sentence.

1. 

Sam is thinking.

2. 

Pam is drinking.

3. 

Frank is winking.

4. 

Ed is singing.

5. 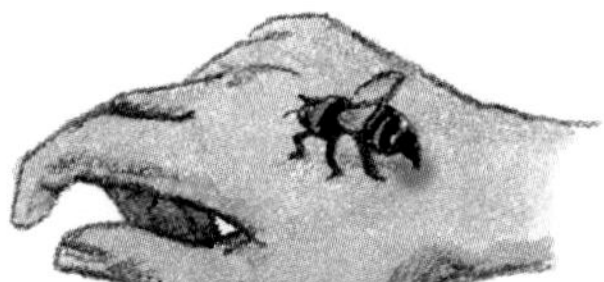

A bee is stinging.

6. 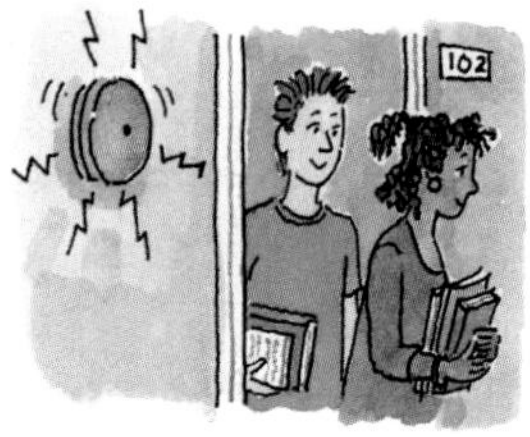

The bell is ringing.

6 Read and Write Look at the picture. Write the missing word.

swim thin grin ~~twins~~

1. Bill and Phil are ___twins___.

2. They are both ________.

3. They have the same ________.

4. They both like to ________.

7 Make Words

A. Change the underlined letters in each word. Make new words. Use the letters below.

-ill -in -ip -ick -ink -ing

1. pack pill ______________________
2. shell ______________________
3. thin ______________________
4. sad ______________________
5. wet ______________________
6. still ______________________

B. Share your words with your classmates.

8 Make Sentences

Choose one word from the unit. Write a sentence.

____.

9 Chant

Listen to the chant. Repeat. Point to each body part.

Head and shoulders, nose and chin
Legs and arms, knees and shins
Eyes and ears, mouth and lips
Waist and stomach, ribs and hips

4 Let's Have Fun!

Short vowels /ŏ/ and /ŭ/

1 Look and Listen Listen and read. Point your thumb up if you think it is fun. Point your thumb down if you think it is not.

1. 

It is fun to shop.

2. 

It is fun to chop logs.

3. 

It is fun to play the drums.

4. 

It is fun to lie in the sun.

5. 

It is fun to mop the floor.

6. 

It is fun to jog or run.

2 See It, Say It Sound out each word.

1. 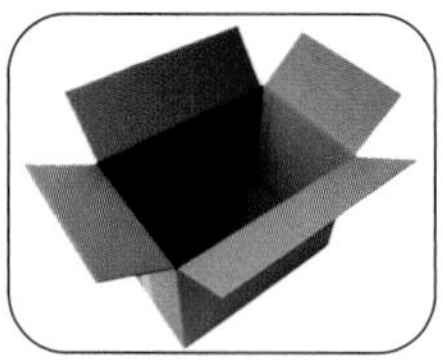

box

2. 

dot

3. 

dog

4. 

rug

5. 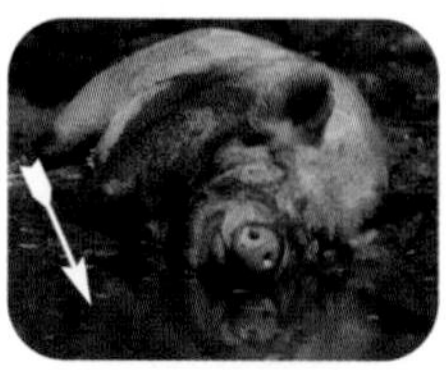

mud

6. 

King Tut

3 Listen and Read Listen. Circle the word you hear.

1.	not	(nut)
2.	dock	duck
3.	rob	rub
4.	cot	cut
5.	sock	suck
6.	hot	hut

4 Figure It Out Match the picture to the correct word.

__d__ 1. cup

_____ 2. lock

_____ 3. stop

_____ 4. study

_____ 5. jump

_____ 6. subtract

a. 

b. 

c. 

~~d~~. 

e. 

f. 10 − 7 = 3

5 Shared Reading Help your teacher read each sentence.

1. 

I can listen to songs.

2. 

I can sing a song.

3. 

I can set a clock.

4. 

I can drive a truck.

5. 

I can play the drums.

6. 

I can smell a skunk.

6 Read and Write Look at the picture. Write the missing word.

rock bus ~~hop~~ stop

1. Scott likes hip __hop__.

2. His sister likes ________.

3. Russ is on the ________.

4. He will get off at the next ________.

7 Make Words

A. Change the underlined letters in each word. Make new words. Use the letters below.

-us -ug -uck -un -ock -ump

1. so<u>ng</u> suck ______________________
2. b<u>oss</u> ______________________
3. r<u>ob</u> ______________________
4. t<u>op</u> ______________________
5. j<u>og</u> ______________________
6. d<u>og</u> ______________________

B. Share your words with your classmates.

8 Make Sentences

Choose one word from the unit. Write a sentence.

____.

9 Chant

Listen to the chant. Repeat.

Let's have fun.
Jog, shop, lie in the sun.
Let's have fun.
Play a game, walk, or run.
Let's have fun.
Toss a ball, play a drum.
Let's have fun.

5 I Do It Every Day!

▷ Long vowel /ā/

1 Look and Listen Listen and read along. Point your thumb up if you do this every day. Point your thumb down if you do not.

1.

wake up late

2.

wash your face

3.

bake a cake

4.

shave

5.

wave to my friends

6.

play a game

7.

take the train

8.

send email

9.

make dinner

2 Listen and Read Listen. Circle the word you hear.

1.	pal	pail
2.	back	bake
3.	Jan	Jane
4.	snack	snake
5.	pan	pain
6.	pants	paints

pail

snake

pain

3 Figure It Out Match the picture to the correct word.

c 1. whale

___ 2. brain

___ 3. pay

___ 4. plate

___ 5. vase

a. 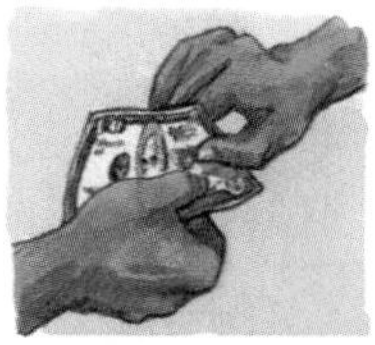

b. 

c. 

d. 

e. 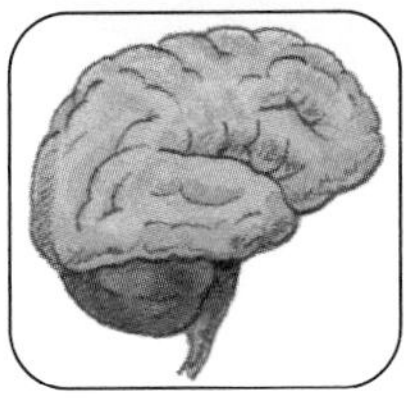

4 Shared Reading Help your teacher read each sentence.

1.

I wake up at 6:30.

2.

I wash my face.

3.

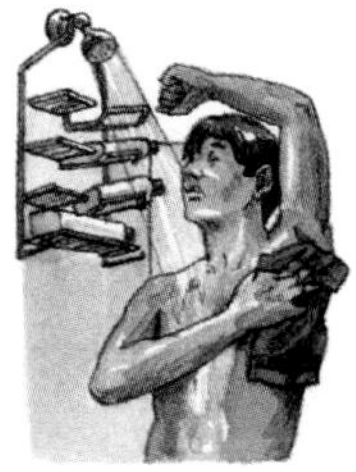

I take a shower.

4.

I make my lunch.

5.

I take the train.

6.

I play a video game.

5 Read and Write Look at the picture. Write the missing word.

make   late   email   face

1. Nina wakes up ________ every morning.

2. Ted washes his ________ in the morning.

3. Susan sends ________ every afternoon.

4. Alex likes to ________ dinner on Mondays.

6 Make Words

A. Change the underlined letters in each word. Make new words. Use the letters below.

-ane -ame -ate -ace -ay -ain -ail

1. d<u>ance</u> date ____________________
2. pl<u>an</u> ____________________
3. l<u>ap</u> ____________________
4. s<u>ack</u> ____________________
5. tr<u>ash</u> ____________________
6. m<u>ath</u> ____________________

B. Share your words with your classmates.

7 Make Sentences

Choose one word from the unit. Write a sentence.

____________________.

8 Chant

Listen to the chant. Repeat.

Rain, rain, go away.
We have a baseball game to play!
We have a race we want to run.
The sky is gray . . . Hey, where's the sun?
Rain, rain, go away.
Come again another day.

6 I See Animals!

Long vowel /ē/

1 Look and Listen

Point your thumb up if the animal scares you. Point your thumb down if it does not.

1. 
bee

2. 
sheep

3. 
parakeet

4. 
eel

5. 
cheetah

6. 
chimpanzee

7. 
seal

8. 
eagle

2 See It, Say It

Sound out each word.

1. 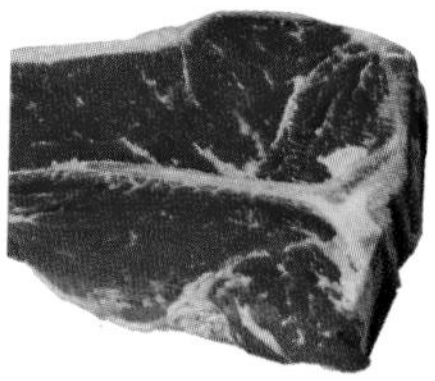
meat

2. 
street

3. 
geese

4. 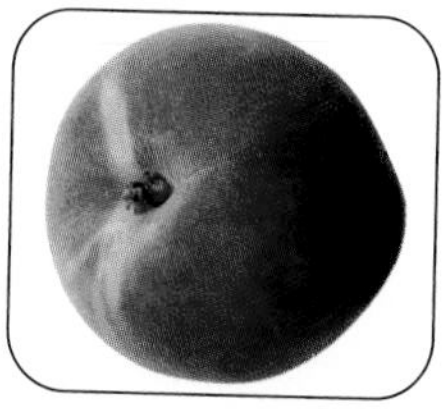
peach

5. 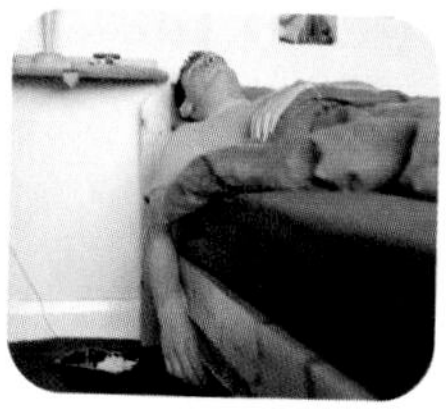
sleep

6. 
leaf

3 Listen and Read Listen. Circle the word you hear.

1.	shape	sheep
2.	wake	week
3.	Jane	Jean
4.	sail	seal
5.	mail	meal
6.	fail	feel

meal

fail

4 Figure It Out Match the picture to the correct word.

_____ 1. bleed

_____ 2. feet

_____ 3. green

_____ 4. meat

_____ 5. beach

a. 

b. 

c. 

d. 

e. 

5 Shared Reading Help your teacher read each sentence.

1. 

A chimpanzee squeals.

2. 

An eagle screeches.

3. 

A parakeet tweets.

4. 

A cheetah screams.

5. 

A chick cheeps.

6. 

A sheep bleats.

6 Read and Write Look at the picture. Write the missing word.

peaches ~~eats~~ cheese meat

1. A shark eats fish.

2. A mouse eats ________.

3. A cheetah eats ________.

4. I love to eat ________.

7 Make Words

A. Change the underlined letters in each word. Make new words. Use the letters below.

-eet	-eed	-eel	-eek	-eem	-eech	-eep
-eat	-ead	-eal	-eak	-eam	-each	-eap

1. b<u>et</u> beet ____________________
2. s<u>et</u> ____________________
3. r<u>est</u> ____________________
4. f<u>ed</u> ____________________
5. m<u>en</u> ____________________
6. t<u>en</u> ____________________

B. Share your words with your classmates.

8 Make Sentences

Choose one word from the unit. Write a sentence.

____.

9 Chant

Listen to the chant. Repeat.

It begins with *sh-*
And it ends with *-eep*.
Put them together,
It's a sheep!

It begins with *b-*
And it ends with *-ee*.
Put them together,
It's a bee!

7 Everyone Likes Mike!

▷ Long vowel /ī/

1 Look and Listen Everyone likes Mike. Point your thumb up 👍 if the sentence is probably true. Point your thumb down 👎 if it is not.

1. 

Mike is bright.

2. 

Mike likes to fight.

3. 

Mike is polite.

4. 

Mike is nice.

5. 

Mike has a wide smile.

6. 

Mike is shy.

2 See It, Say It Sound out each word.

1. 

dime

2. 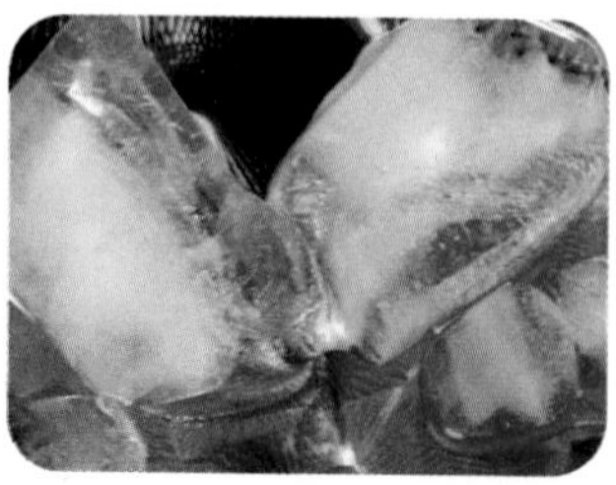

ice

3. 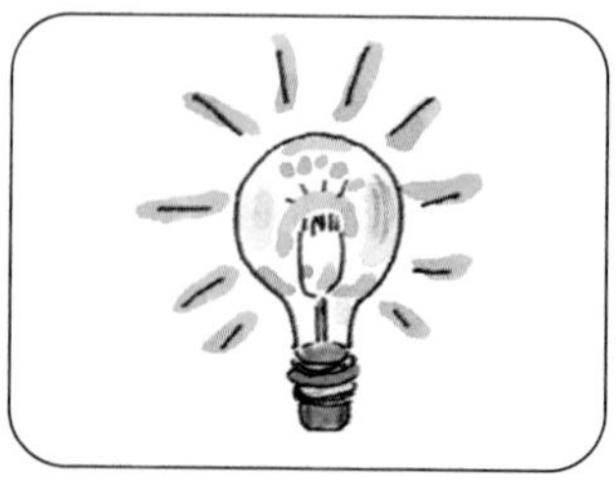

light

3 Listen and Read Listen. Circle the word you hear.

1.	seed	side
2.	bee	by
3.	weed	wide
4.	beat	bite
5.	feet	fight
6.	team	time

weed

beat

4 Figure It Out Match the picture to the correct word.

_____ 1. write

_____ 2. line

_____ 3. rice

_____ 4. dime

_____ 5. knife

a. 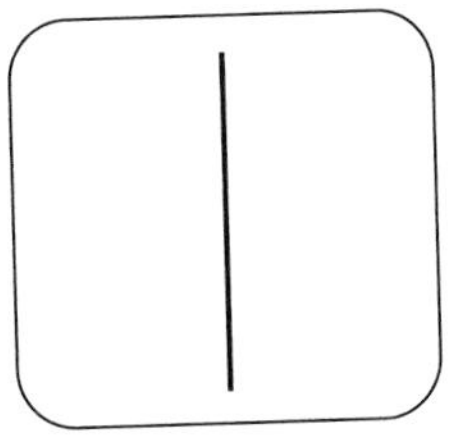

b. 

c. 

d. 

e. 

5 Shared Reading Help your teacher read each sentence.

1. Mike is taking a five-mile hike.

2. Mike is learning to dive.

3. Mike is learning to drive.

4. Mike is learning to tie a tie.

6 Read and Write Mike and Spike are opposites. Look at the picture. Write the missing word.

write   lie   fight

1. Mike is nice.
   Spike likes to ________.

2. Mike likes to read.
   Spike likes to ________.

3. Mike always tells the truth. Spike likes to ________.

7 Make Words

A. Change the underlined letters in each word. Make new words. Use the letters below.

-ice -ide -ime -ine -ite -ive -ight

1. feet fine ______________________
2. leak ______________________
3. neat ______________________
4. team ______________________
5. sleep ______________________
6. read ______________________

B. Share your words with your classmates.

8 Make Sentences

Choose one word from the unit. Write a sentence.

____.

9 Chant

Listen to the chant. Repeat.

Friends, friends 1, 2, 3.
My best friend sits right next to me.
His name is Mike!
He's funny, he's bright.
He likes to smile and he's polite.
I'll say it once, I'll say it twice.
Friends, friends 1, 2, 3.
My best friend sits right next to me.

8 Let's Go to the Grocery Store.

Long vowels /ō/, /ū/, and /o͞o/

1 Look and Listen Point your thumb up if this is at the grocery store. Point your thumb down if it is not.

1.

roast beef

2.

toads

3.

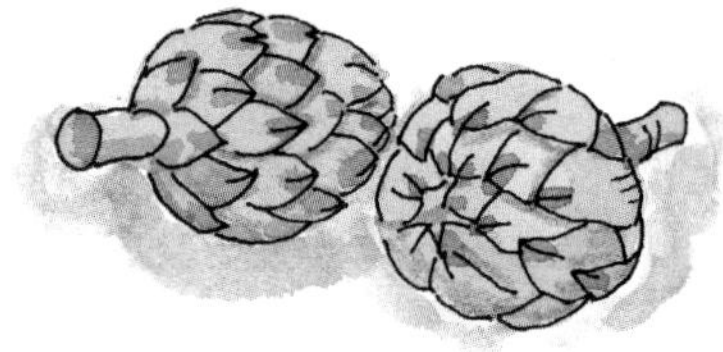

artichokes

4.

low fat yogurt

5.

chicken noodle soup

6.

mushrooms

7.

tools

8.

menu

9.

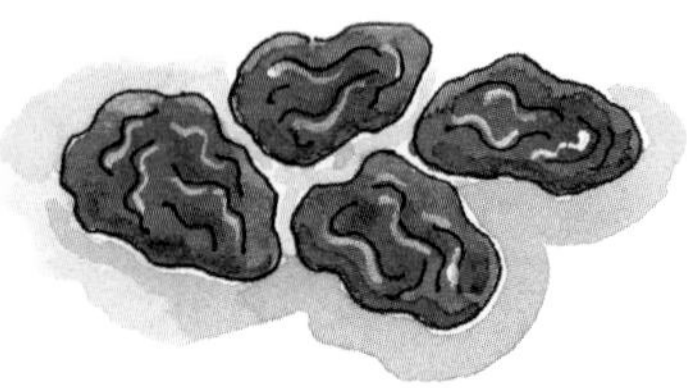

a few prunes

② See It, Say It Sound out each word.

1. 

ice cubes

2. 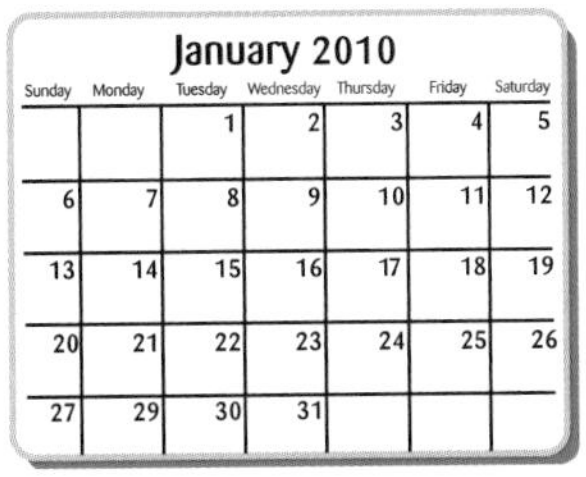

January

3. 

toast

4. 

coat

5. 

boot

6. 

fruit

③ Figure It Out Match the picture to the correct word.

_____ 1. phone

_____ 2. globe

_____ 3. computer

_____ 4. ruler

_____ 5. noon

a. 

b. 

c. 

d. 

e. 

4 Shared Reading Help your teacher read each sentence.

1. 

Get a loaf of bread.

2. 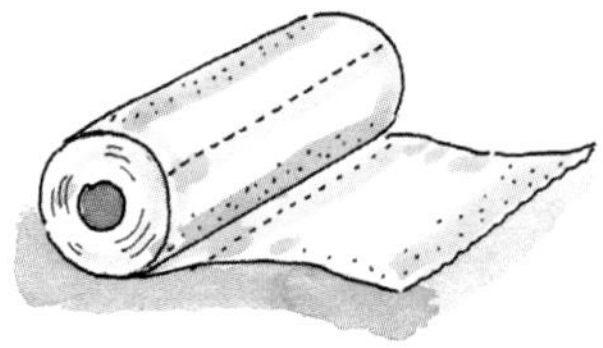

Get a roll of paper towels.

3. 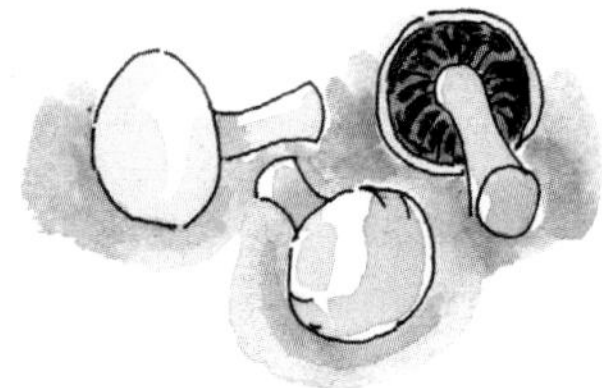

Get a few mushrooms.

4. 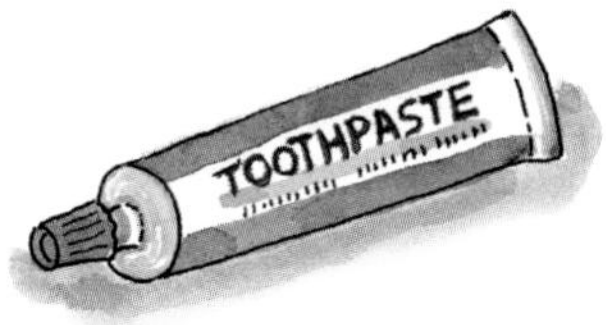

Get a tube of toothpaste.

5. 

Get a package of frozen corn.

6. 

Get a can of tuna.

5 Read and Write Look at the picture. Write the missing word.

noodle roast loaf toast

1. It's time for breakfast. I'd like eggs and ________.

2. I'd like chicken ________ soup for lunch.

3. It's time for dinner! Would you like ________ beef . . . ?

4. . . . or meat ________?

6 Make Words

A. Change the underlined letters in each word. Make new words. Use the letters below.

-oat -oad -oast -ose -ool -oot -ube

1. tune ______________________
2. coal ______________________
3. boom ______________________
4. soap ______________________
5. robe ______________________
6. noon ______________________

B. Share your words with your classmates.

7 Make Sentences

Choose one word from the unit. Write a sentence.

____.

8 Chant

Listen to the chant. Repeat.

I like to eat
I like to eat
Artichokes
With eggs and toast,
Hot roast beef,
And Mom's meatloaf.
What do you like to eat?

1 I Like Hip Hop!

A Connecting to Your Life

1 Talk It Over Walk around your classroom. Find someone who likes each type of music. Write the person's name on the line.

hip hop

____

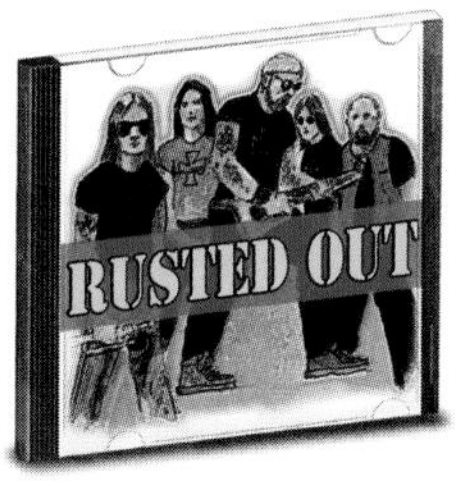

rock

____

pop

____

R&B

____

classical

____

country

____

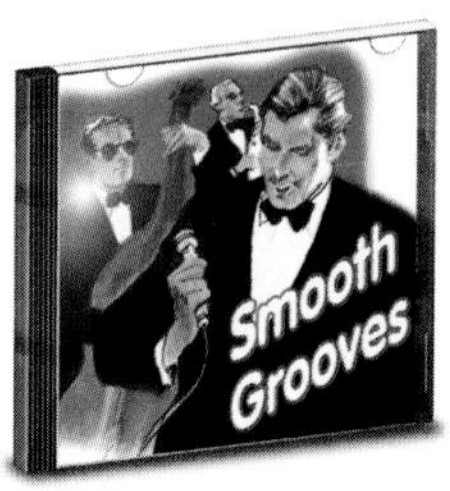

jazz

____

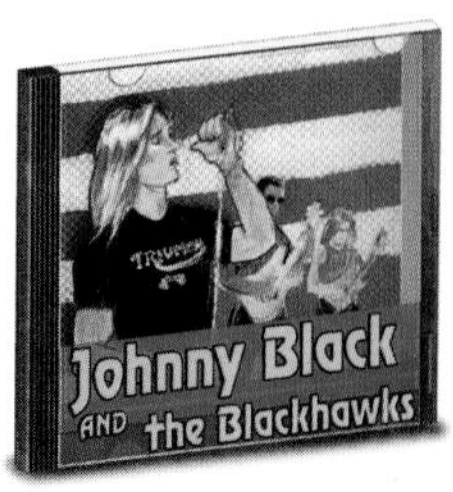

heavy metal

____

salsa

____

② Do It

A. Look at the CD covers again. Circle the kind of music you like best.

B. Complete this sentence. Share with a partner.

My favorite kind of music is ________________________________.

C. Help your teacher make a graph that shows your classmates' favorite kinds of music.

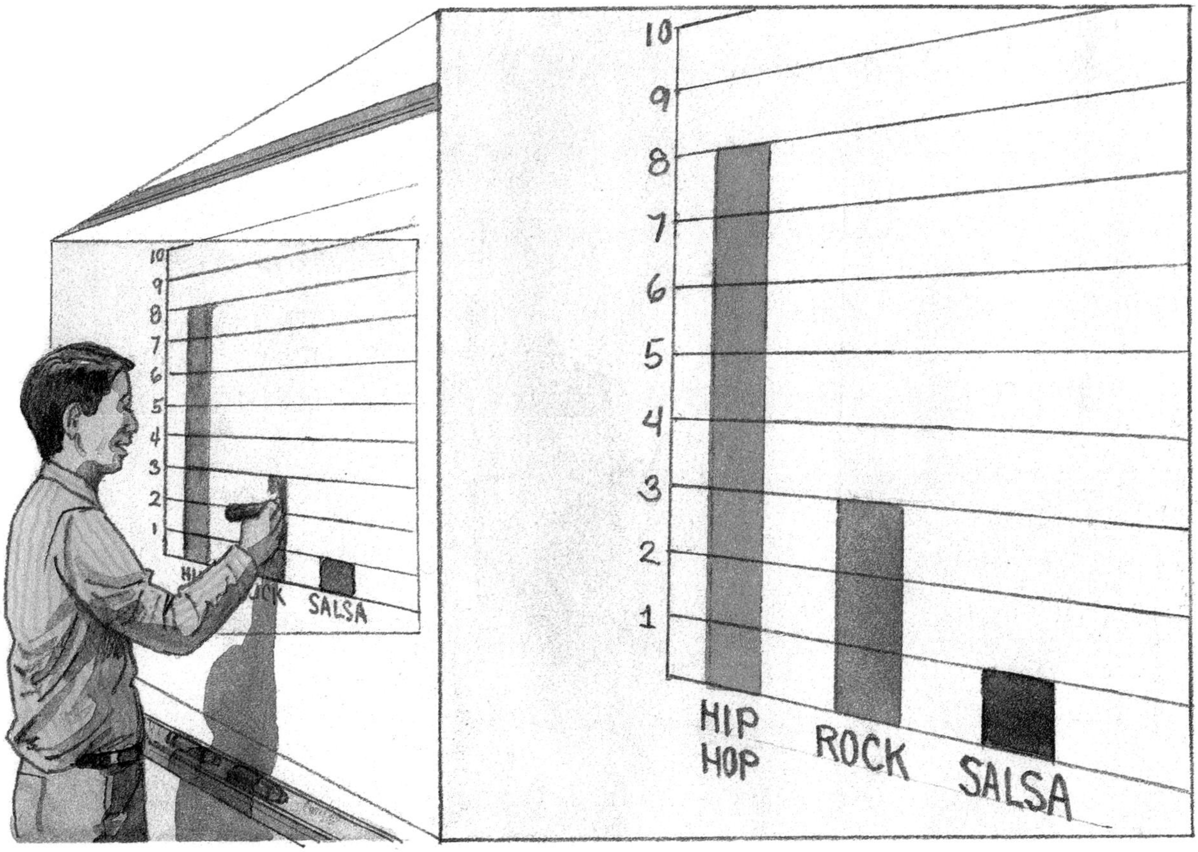

B Reading

1 Let's Read Tran and Maria made a Venn diagram. Their Venn diagram shows the kinds of movies they like.

A. Listen. Read the diagram.

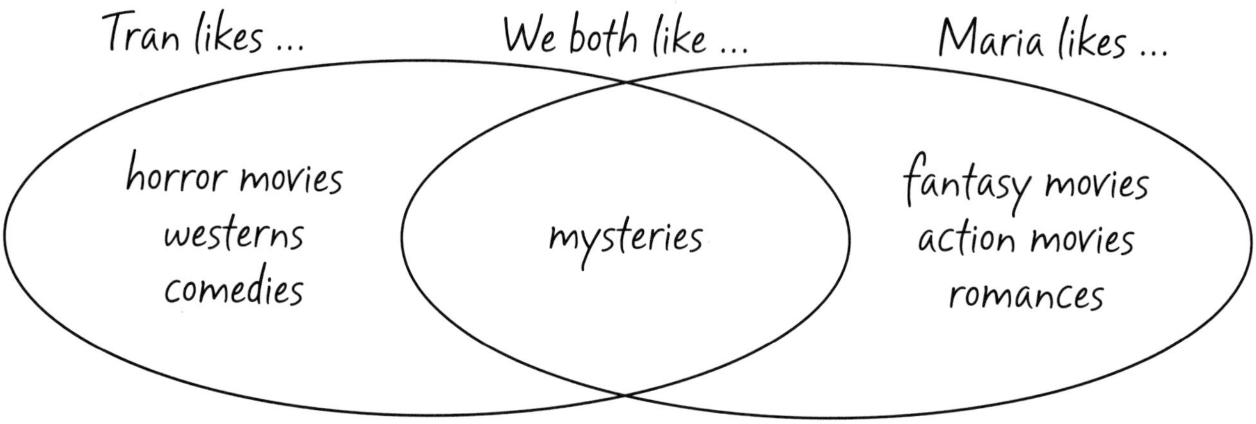

horror

western

comedy

mystery

fantasy

action

romance

B. Read what Tran wrote about the Venn diagram.

I like horror movies, westerns, and comedies.
My partner Maria likes fantasy movies, action movies, and romances.
We both like mysteries.

❷ Unlock Meaning

Read each sentence. Write *T* if the sentence is true. Write *F* if it is false.

T 1. Tran likes horror movies.

_____ 2. Tran and Maria both like action movies.

_____ 3. Maria likes westerns.

_____ 4. Maria likes fantasy movies.

_____ 5. Tran and Maria both like mysteries.

_____ 6. Tran likes comedies.

❸ Build Fluency

Listen. Work with a partner. Take turns reading the students' words.

I like hip hop.
So do I.
I like pop.
Not me.
I like salsa.
I do, too!

❹ Talk about It

A. List the titles of three movies you like.

____

____

____

B. Share with a partner. Tell about the three movies you like.

C Phonics

1 See It, Say It Listen to each word. Say each word aloud. Listen to the plural -s.

cabs

dogs

beds

socks

pets

cuffs

2 Learn the Rule

Add -s to most nouns to make them plural. When you add the plural -s to words that end in the sounds /p/, /t/, /k/, and /f/, the -s sounds like /s/.

With vowel sounds and most other consonant sounds, the plural -s sounds like /z/. (See page 108 for more information about plural nouns.)

3 Fun with Words Listen to each word. Write the word in the correct column.

Sounds like /**s**/	Sounds like /**z**/
	movies

1. movies

2. books

3. TV shows

4. sports

5. singers

D Grammar

1 Talk to Others Listen to the dialog. Act it out.

Juan: **I** like hip hop.

Lori: **I** do, too! **We** both like hip hop!

Juan: Do **you** like pop?

Lori: No, but my mother does. **She** likes pop.

Juan: What about your father?

Lori: **He** likes pop, too. **They** both like pop.

2 Learn the Rule A subject pronoun takes the place of a noun. Subject pronouns can be singular or plural.

SUBJECT PRONOUNS					
Singular			Plural		
Subject	Verb	Object	Subject	Verb	Object
I	like	hip hop.	**We**	like	hip hop.
You	like	hip hop.	**You**	like	hip hop.
He	likes	hip hop.	**They**	like	hip hop.
She	likes	hip hop.			
It	likes	dog treats.			

3 Practice Complete each sentence. Write the correct subject pronoun.

1. Juan and I like music. ___We___ both like country.
2. Mary likes TV. ____________ likes to watch football.
3. Juan and Lori like movies. ____________ both like mysteries.
4. My father likes funny movies. ____________ likes comedies.
5. I like to read. ____________ like books about animals.
6. Do you like music? What kind of music do ____________ like?

E Content Connections

1 Let's Read Read about gorillas and chimpanzees.

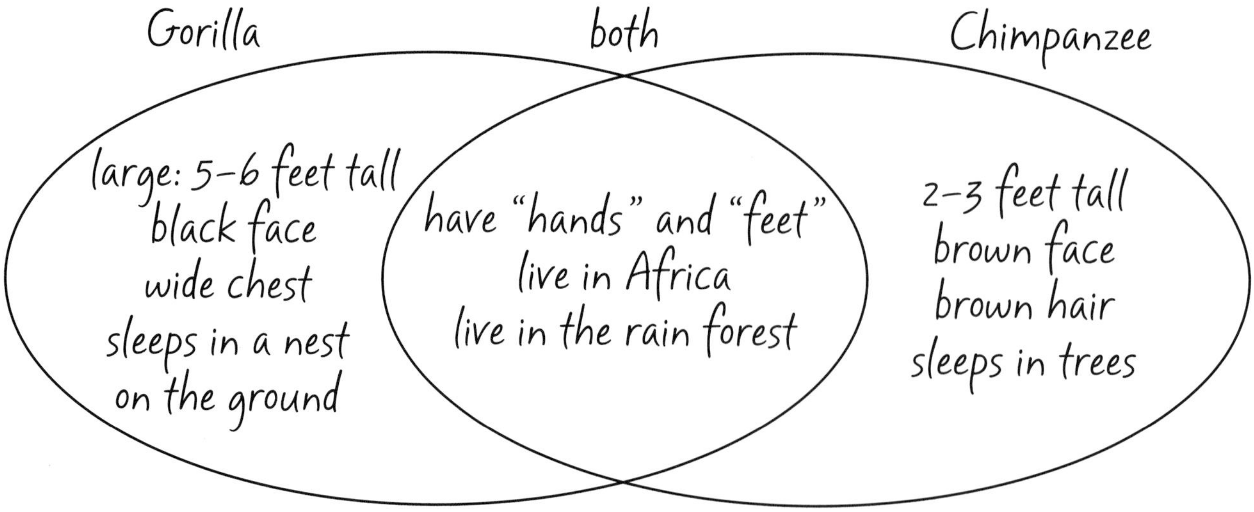

2 On Your Own Complete each sentence. Use the words below.

feet | large | rain forest | ~~Africa~~ | trees | chest

1. Gorillas and chimpanzees live on the same continent. They live in Africa.
2. A gorilla is 5 to 6 feet tall. It is very ____________.
3. A gorilla has a wide ___________.
4. Gorillas and chimpanzees both have hands and _________.
5. Gorillas and chimpanzees both live in the ________________.
6. Chimpanzees sleep in ____________.

3 Think about It Look carefully at the pictures of the alligators and the crocodiles. Complete the Venn diagram.

large reptiles; live in water; eat meat; live in the southeastern U.S. and parts of China; wide, short snouts; grayish black color.

large reptiles; live in water; eat meat; live all over the world; long, narrow snouts; light tan color.

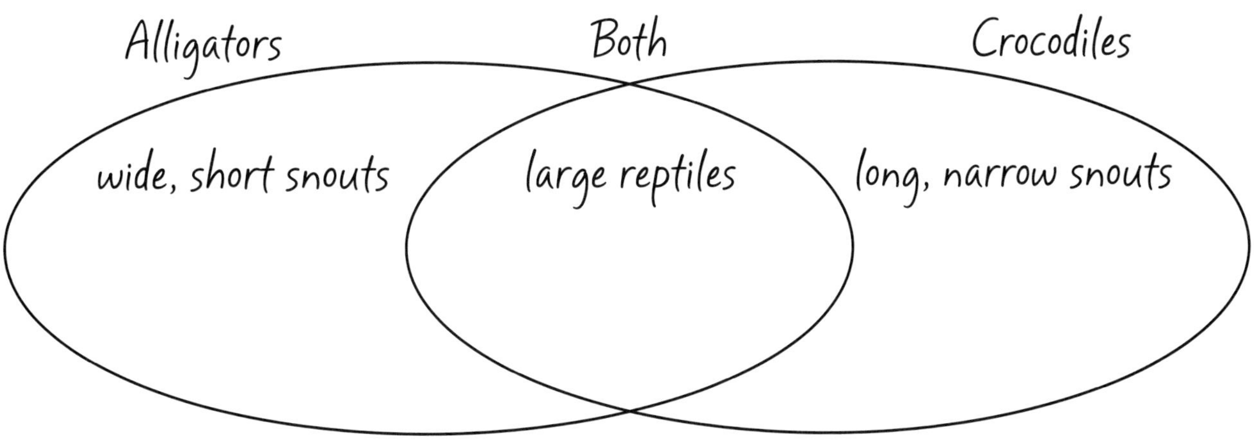

F Writing

Work with a partner. Make a Venn diagram. Compare the TV shows you like.

1 Getting It Out

A. On your own, circle the kinds of TV shows you like.

news

sitcoms

game shows

cartoons

nature shows

police dramas

talk shows

soap operas

sports

B. Talk with a partner. Do you like the same kinds of shows?

2 Getting It Down

A. On a piece of paper, make a Venn diagram that tells which kinds of shows each of you likes. Use pencil.

B. On your own, write three sentences about your Venn diagram.

3 Getting It Right Read your Venn diagram aloud to each other. Talk it over. Make changes if you want to.

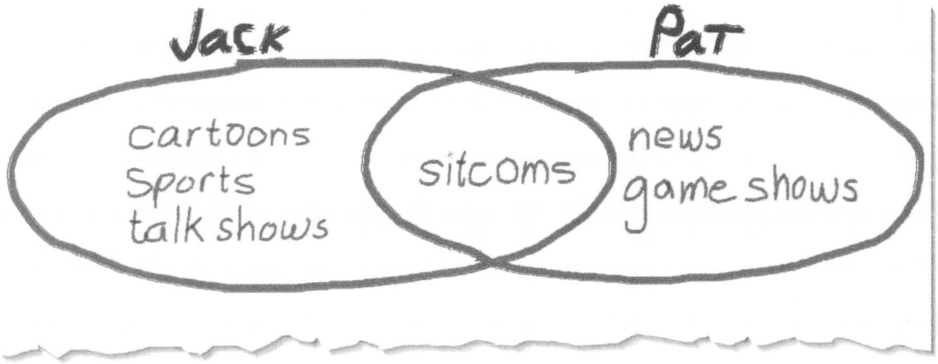

4 Presenting It Show your Venn diagram to your classmates.

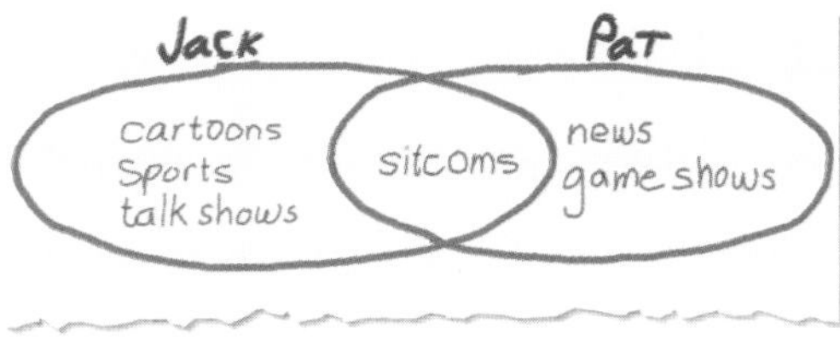

2 This Is My Family Tree.

A Connecting to Your Life

1 Talk It Over Work with a partner. Look at the picture of Matt's family. Label each person.

Family Words

father	mother	grandfather
grandmother	sister	brother
aunt	uncle	cousin

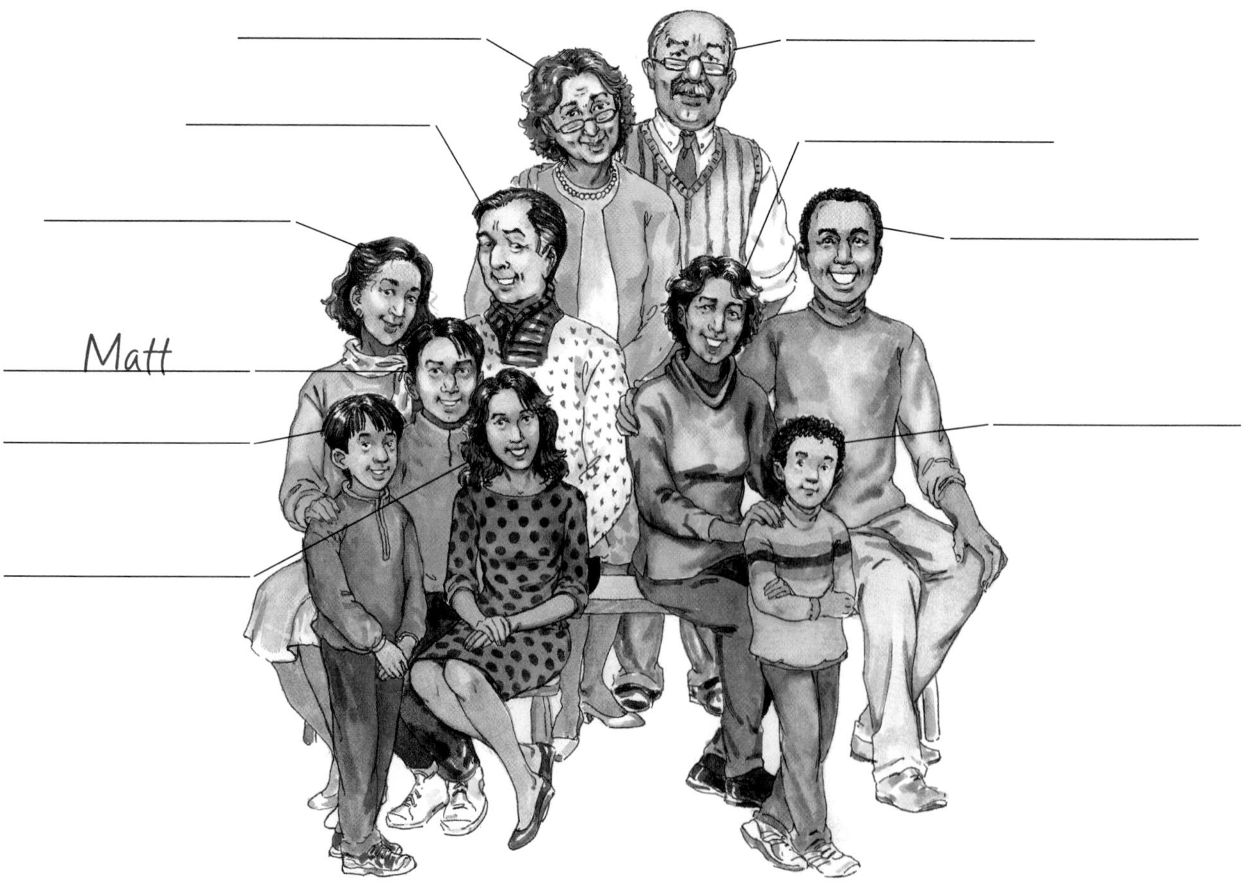

❷ Do It

A. Draw a picture of your own family.

B. Introduce your family. Complete the sentences.

1. This is my ______________________________.
2. This is ______________________________.
3. This ______________________________.

C. Talk to a partner. Compare your families.

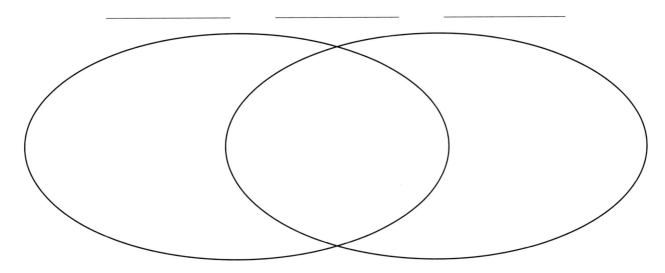

______________ ______________ ______________

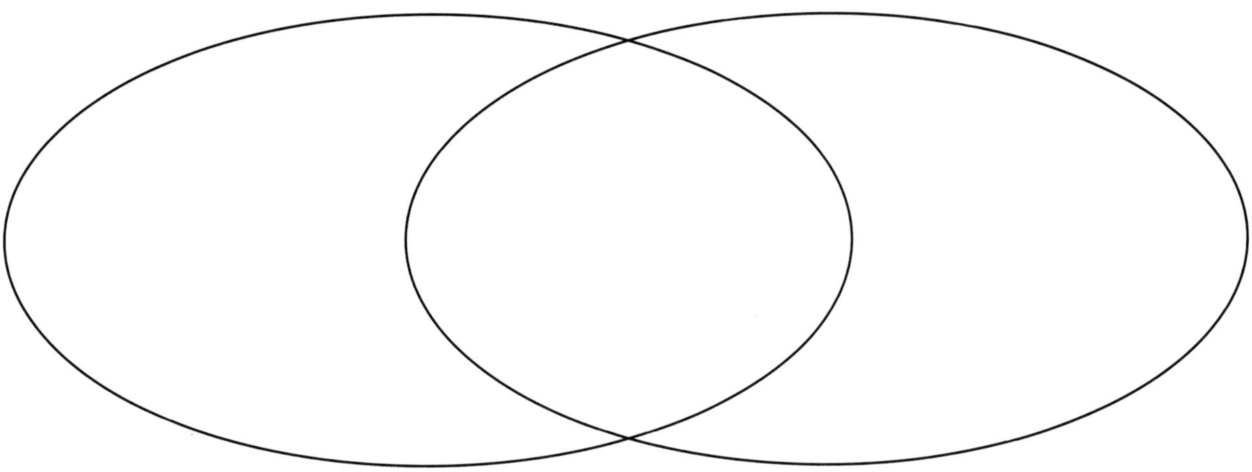

B Reading

1 Let's Read Jenny made a family tree.

A. Look at Jenny's family tree. Listen. Read the names.

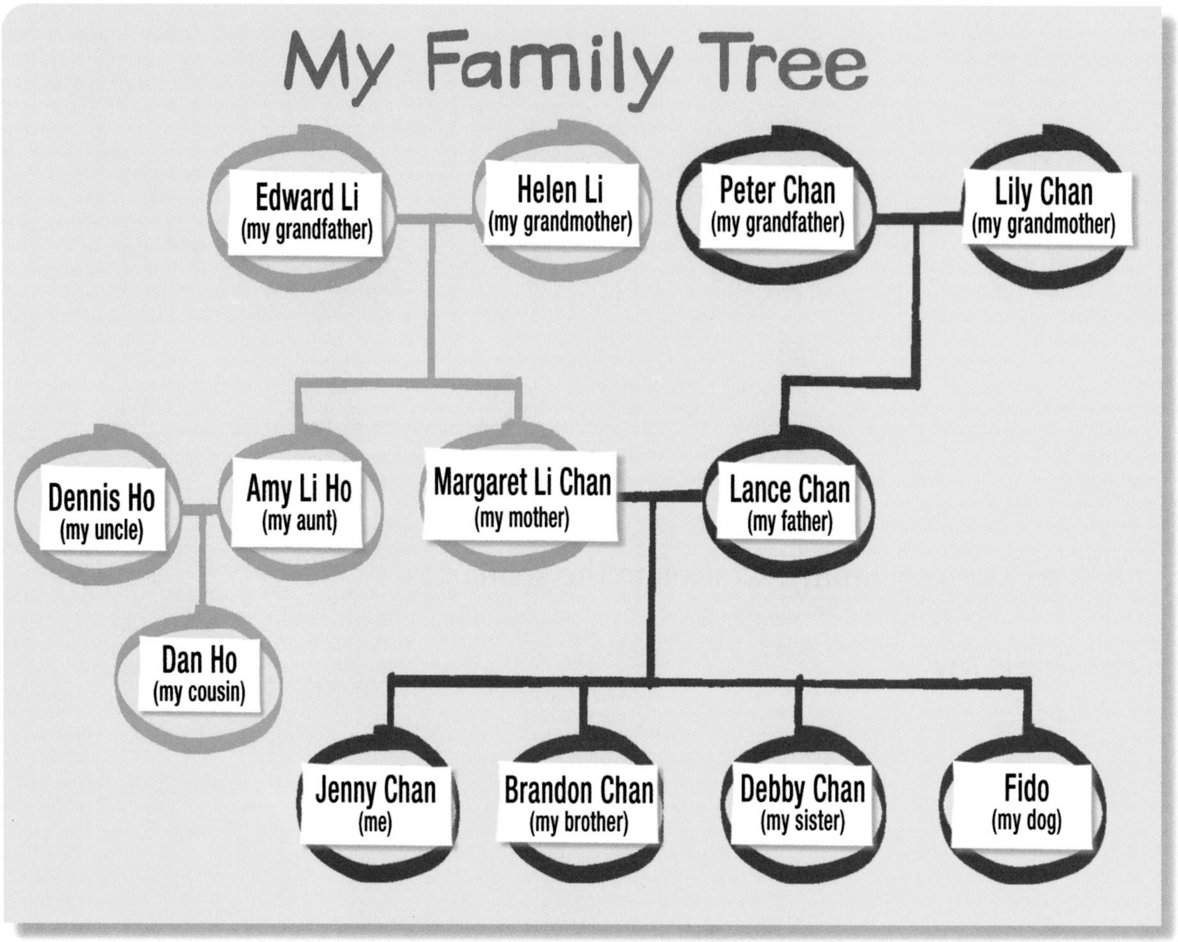

B. Read what Jenny wrote about her family.

This is my family tree. I have one brother and one sister. I also have a dog.

2 Unlock Meaning Match each of Jenny's family members to his or her name.

__c__	1. Debby Chan	a.	uncle
____	2. Dennis Ho	b.	brother
____	3. Peter Chan	c.	sister
____	4. Dan Ho	d.	father
____	5. Amy Ho	e.	aunt
____	6. Margaret Chan	f.	grandfather
____	7. Lance Chan	g.	cousin
____	8. Brandon Chan	h.	mother

3 Build Fluency Listen. Work with a partner. Read the dialog.

Jenny: This is my sister. Her name is Debby.
Juan: This is my brother. His name is Pablo.
Jenny: This is my mother. Her name is Margaret.
Juan: This is my father. His name is Roberto.
Jenny: This is my aunt. Her name is Amy.
Juan: This is my uncle. His name is David.
Jenny: This is my grandmother. Her name is Lily.
Juan: This is my grandfather. His name is Miguel.

4 Talk about It Talk with a partner. Ask and answer two questions about your families.

Example:

A: Do you have any sisters or brothers?

B: I have a sister and a brother.

A: What are their names?

B: My sister's name is Jessica. My brother's name is Jake.

C Phonics

1 See It, Say It

Listen to each word. Say each word aloud.

house

round

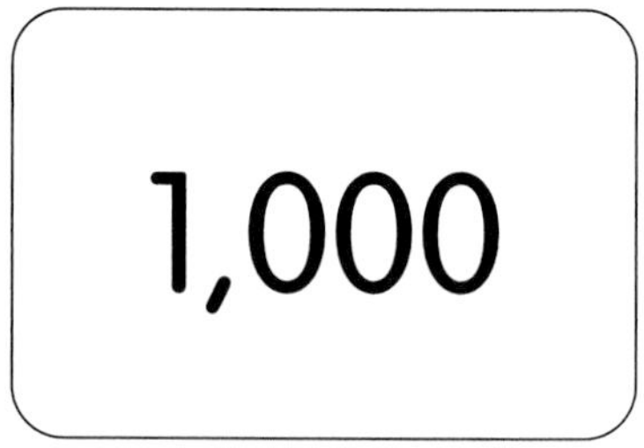

thousand

touch

rough

double

2 Learn the Rule

Sometimes the letters **ou** sound like br**ow**n.

Sometimes the letters **ou** sound like f**u**n.

3 Fun with Words

Listen to each word. Write the word in the correct column.

Sounds like **brown**	Sounds like **fun**
	country

1. country

2. mouse

3. mouth

4. cousin

5. couple

D Grammar

1 Talk to Others Listen to the dialog. Act it out.

Juan: Is this **your** brother?

Jenny: Yes. **His** name is Brandon.

Juan: Is this **your** sister?

Jenny: Yes. **Her** name is Debby.

Juan: Is this **your** mother?

Jenny: No. This is **my** aunt. **Her** name is Amy.

2 Learn the Rule Possessive adjectives show who something belongs to.

SUBJECT PRONOUNS	POSSESSIVE ADJECTIVES
I have a red pen.	This is **my** pen.
You have a blue pen.	This is **your** pen.
He has a pencil.	This is **his** pencil.
She has a pen.	This is **her** pen.
It has a dog house.	This is **its** dog house.
We have the same teacher.	Ms. Lee is **our** teacher.
They have a different teacher.	Mr. Lopez is **their** teacher.

3 Practice Complete each sentence. Use *my, his, her, your, our* or *their.*

1. I have a sister. ___My___ sister is 16.
2. My aunt and uncle have a son. __________ son is my cousin.
3. Lori has a brother. __________ brother is in middle school.
4. You have a cap. __________ cap is really cool.
5. My brother and I have a car. __________ car is blue.
6. My uncle has a dog. __________ dog is brown.

E Content Connections

1 Let's Read Scientists make diagrams. Read the words in the branching diagram.

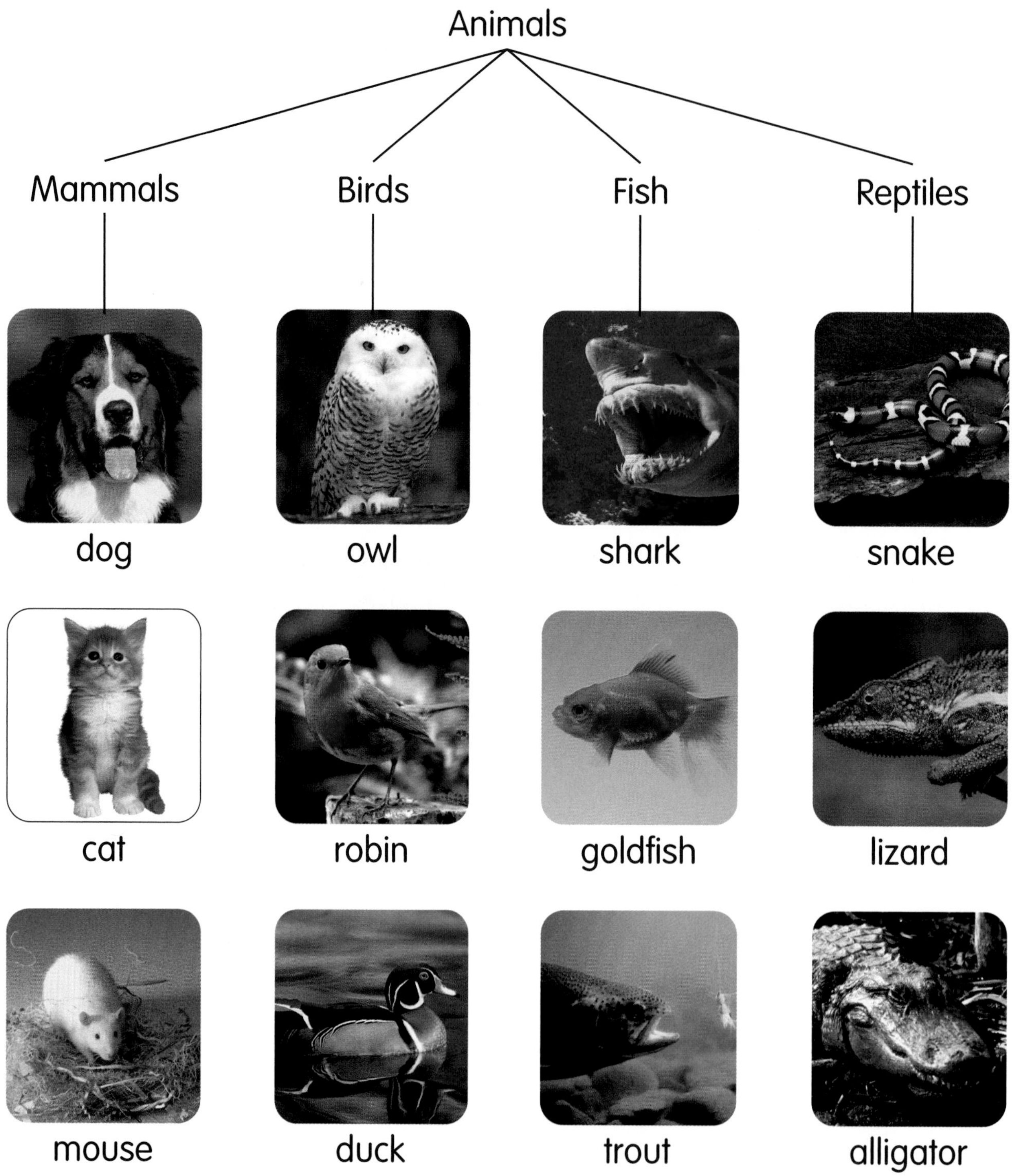

2 On Your Own Complete each sentence with *mammal, bird, fish,* or *reptile.*

1. A dog is a <u>mammal</u>.
2. A shark is a ________.
3. A robin is a ________.
4. A mouse is a ________.
5. A snake is a ________.
6. A trout is a ________.
7. An eagle is a ________.
8. A lizard is a ________.

3 Think about It Complete the diagram. Where does each animal belong?

tuna

duck

monkey

flounder

cow

turtle

eagle

crocodile

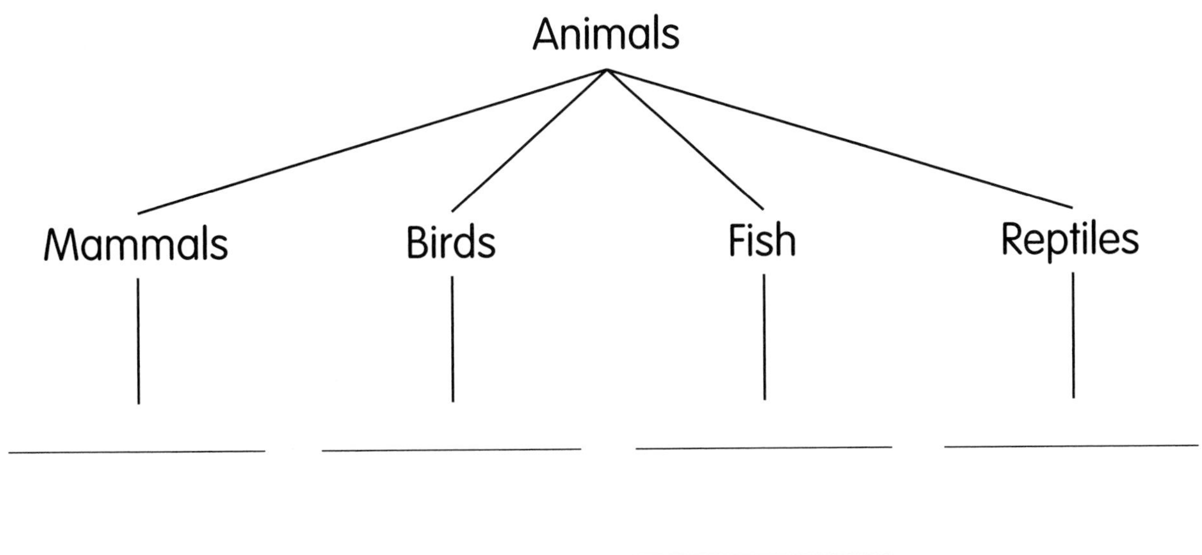

F Writing

Make a family tree. Take out—

a sheet of paper

a ruler

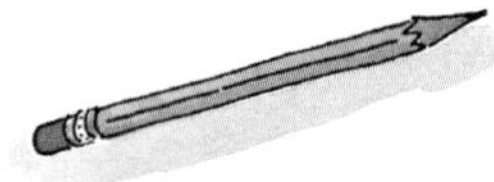

a pencil

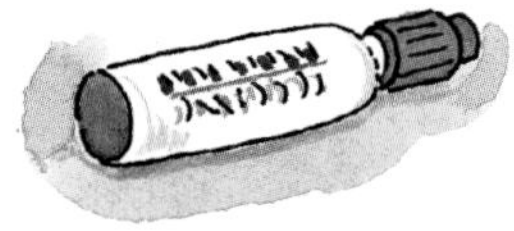

a marker

1 Getting It Out List your family members.

My family

Me: Pam

My grandparents: Juana, José, Marta, Ricardo

My parents: Rosa, Alejandro

My brothers and sisters: Roberto, Juan-Carlos

2 Getting It Down

A. Make your family tree. Use a pencil.

B. Write three sentences about your family.

3 Getting It Right

A. Make corrections.

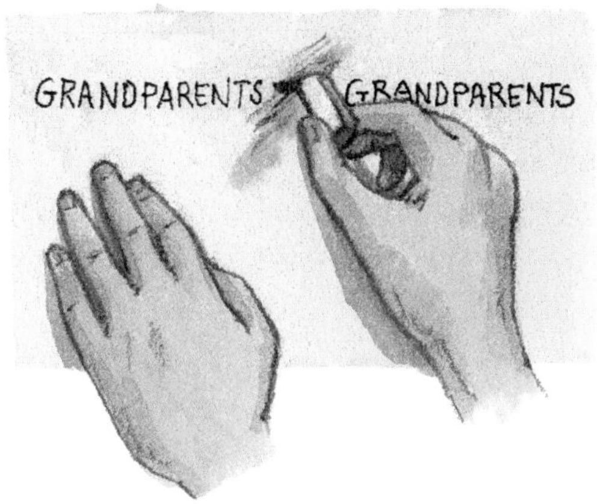

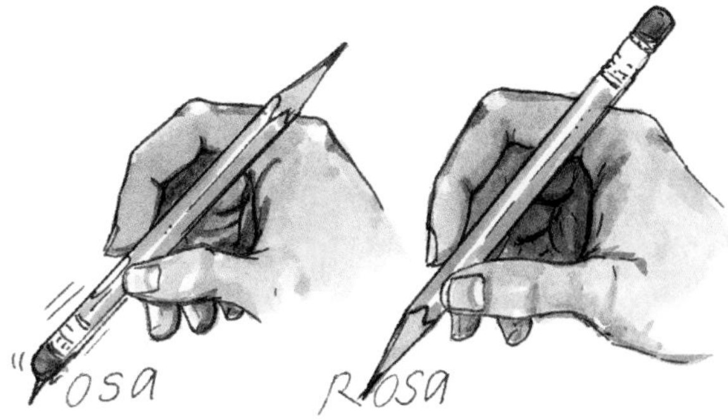

B. Finish your family tree. Use a pen.

4 Presenting It Show your family tree to your classmates.

3 This Is My Life.

A Connecting to Your Life

1 Talk It Over

A. Work with a partner. Juan does these things every day. Put them in time order. Write 1–9 on the lines. Different answers are possible.

_____ a. takes a shower

_____ b. goes to bed

_____ c. eats lunch

_____ d. eats breakfast

_____ e. takes the bus to school

__1__ f. wakes up

_____ g. does his homework

_____ h. has dinner

_____ i. leaves school

B. Tell what Juan does every day.

2 Do It

A. What do you do every day? Make a list.

Wake up ______________________ ______________________

______________________ ______________________

______________________ ______________________

______________________ ______________________

______________________ ______________________

B. Share with a partner. Circle one thing on your list that is not on your partner's list.

C. Make a daily timeline. Write the things you do every day on your timeline.

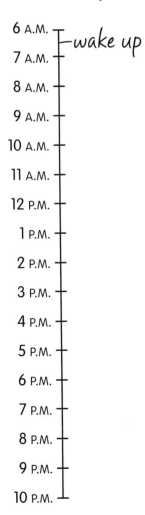

6 A.M. — wake up
7 A.M.
8 A.M.
9 A.M.
10 A.M.
11 A.M.
12 P.M.
1 P.M.
2 P.M.
3 P.M.
4 P.M.
5 P.M.
6 P.M.
7 P.M.
8 P.M.
9 P.M.
10 P.M.

B Reading

1 Let's Read Juan made a timeline of his life. Listen. Read his timeline.

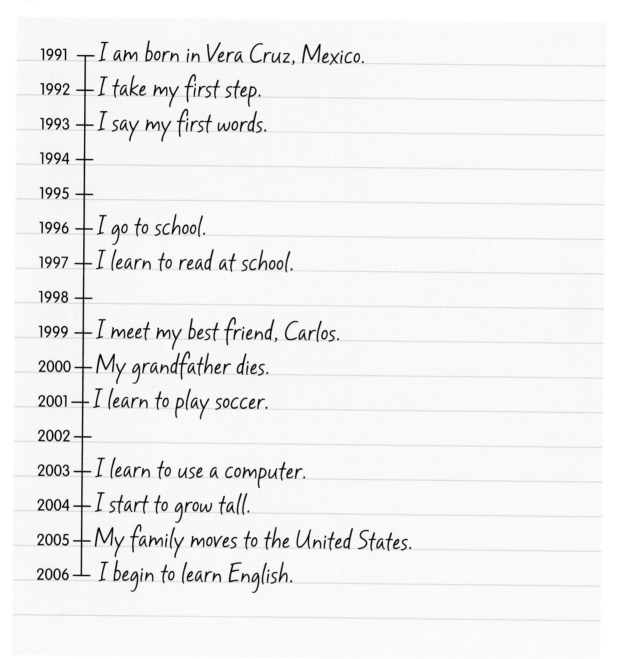

1991 — I am born in Vera Cruz, Mexico.
1992 — I take my first step.
1993 — I say my first words.
1994 —
1995 —
1996 — I go to school.
1997 — I learn to read at school.
1998 —
1999 — I meet my best friend, Carlos.
2000 — My grandfather dies.
2001 — I learn to play soccer.
2002 —
2003 — I learn to use a computer.
2004 — I start to grow tall.
2005 — My family moves to the United States.
2006 — I begin to learn English.

2 Unlock Meaning

Put the events in Juan's timeline in the correct order. Write the numbers 1–7 on the lines.

______ a. Juan's family comes to the United States.

______ b. Juan starts school.

______ c. Juan learns to play soccer.

__1__ d. Juan starts to walk.

______ e. Juan begins to learn English.

______ f. Juan learns to use a computer.

______ g. Juan starts to talk.

3 Build Fluency

Work with a partner.

A. Listen. Read the years aloud in one minute. How many years did you read?

a. 1800	e. 1964	i. 1990	m. 2001
b. 1891	f. 1972	j. 1996	n. 2003
c. 1900	g. 1983	k. 1999	o. 2005
d. 1952	h. 1989	l. 2000	p. 2006

4 Talk about It

A. Think of something important that happened in your life. Draw a picture of what happened.

B. Share with your classmates.

C Phonics

1 See It, Say It

Listen to each word. Say each word aloud.

owl

shower

frown

snow

row

show

2 Learn the Rule

Sometimes the letters **ow** sound like **now**.

Sometimes the letters **ow** sound like **grow**.

3 Fun with Words

Listen to each word. Write the word in the correct column.

Sounds like **now**	Sounds like **grow**
cow	

1. cow

2. blow

3. slow

4. town

5. growl

D Grammar

1 Talk to Others Listen to the dialog. Act it out.

Juan: I like school.
Lori: Me, too. School is fun.
Juan: My favorite subject is math.
Lori: My favorite subject is art. I like drawing and painting.

2 Learn the Rule Nouns, verbs, and adjectives are three important parts of speech.

Nouns name things, people, animals, places, or ideas. They can be singular or plural.

Verbs name actions or states (such as *be, seem, look*).

Adjectives describe nouns or pronouns.

NOUN	VERB	ADJECTIVE	NOUN
Juan	eats	big	lunches.
Lori	paints	pretty	pictures.
Juan	likes	funny	movies.
Lori	has	black	hair.

3 Practice Read each sentence. Write the part of speech of each underlined word.

1. Juan is a <u>student</u>. ____noun____
2. He <u>works</u> hard at school. ________
3. His gets <u>good</u> grades. ________
4. Lori is <u>hungry</u>. ________
5. She <u>loves</u> to eat. ________
6. She likes <u>pizza</u>. ________

E Content Connections

1 Let's Read Timelines teach about history. Read this timeline about inventions of the 20th century.

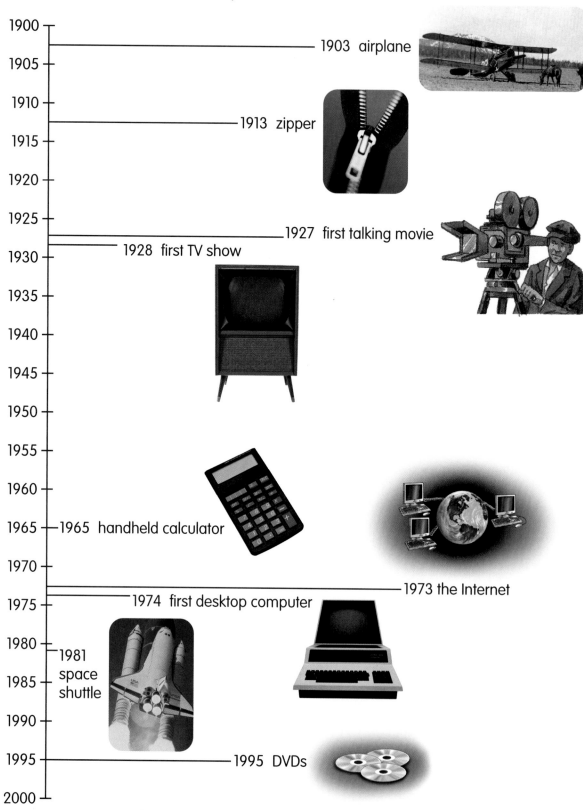

- 1903 airplane

- 1913 zipper

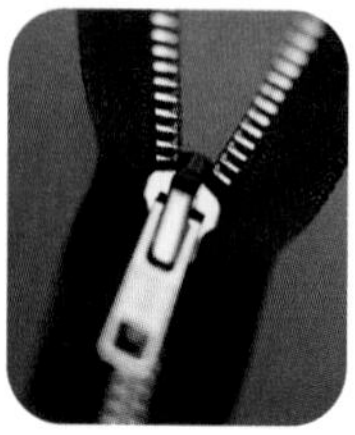

- 1927 first talking movie

- 1928 first TV show

- 1965 handheld calculator

- 1973 the Internet

- 1974 first desktop computer

- 1981 space shuttle

- 1995 DVDs

❷ **On Your Own** Here are three more inventions. Guess when each one was invented. Write the year.

1. cell phone ________

2. credit card ________

3. video games ________

How close were you? Read the answers at the bottom of the page.* Add each invention to the timeline on page 100.

❸ **Think about It** Work with a partner.

A. Decide which inventions are the most important. Rank them 1 (most important) to 10 (least important).

______ a. airplane

______ b. movies

______ c. TV

______ d. calculator

______ e. Internet

______ f. computer

______ g. space shuttle

______ h. cell phone

______ i. credit card

______ j. video game

B. Share with your classmates.

*cell phone: 1973; credit card: 1951; video games: 1958

F Writing

Make a timeline of your life.

1 Getting It Out

A. Write the year you were born. __________

B. Think of things in your life that tell about you: things you did, things you learned, and things that happened to you. Make a list of ten things.

2 Getting It Down Draft your timeline.

A. Draw your timeline. Divide it into equal parts to show how many years you have lived. Use a pencil.

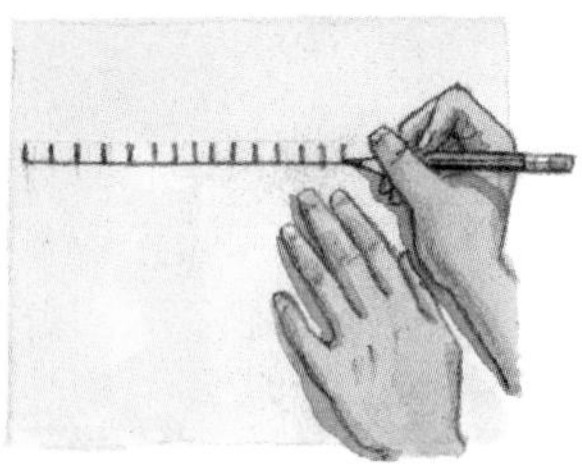

B. Write the years on your timeline. Begin with the year you were born.

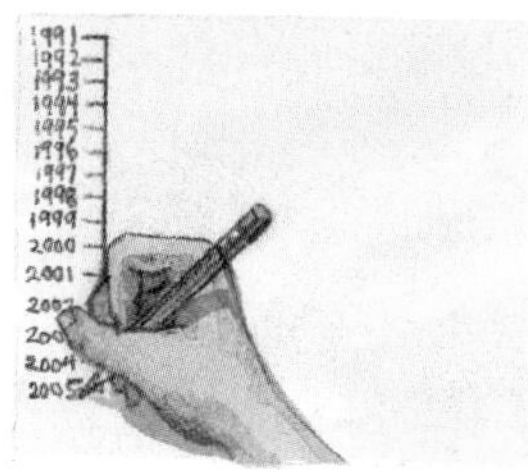

C. Write at least five sentences about yourself.

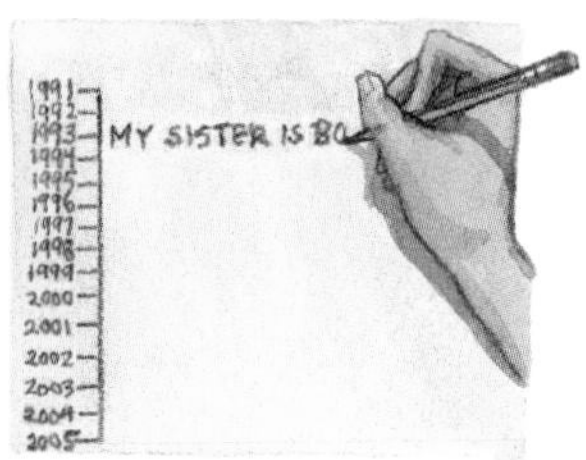

D. Draw a picture of one event on your timeline.

③ Getting It Right

A. Show your timeline to your family. Ask for their ideas.

B. Make corrections.

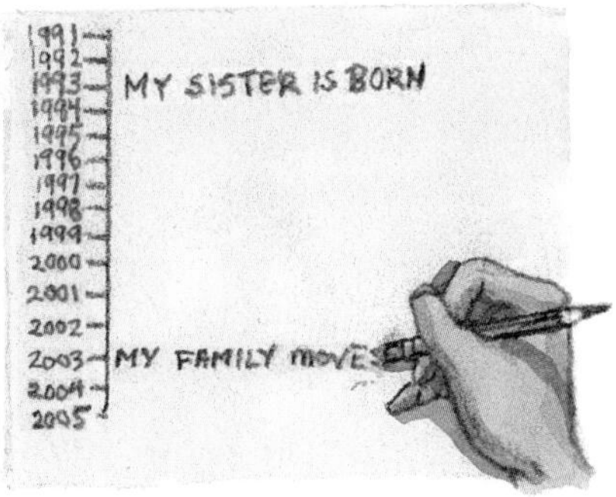

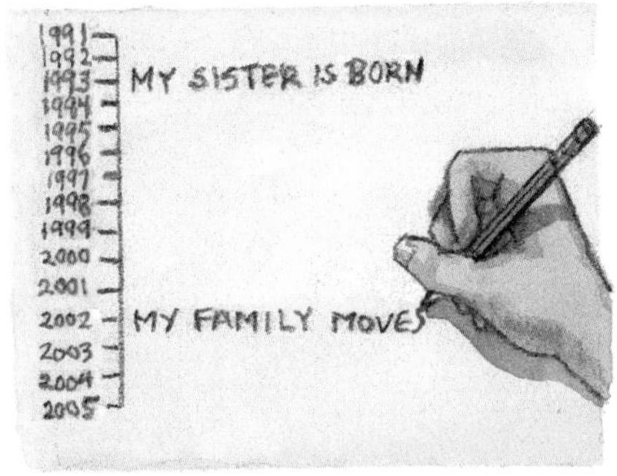

C. Finish your timeline. Use pens and markers.

④ Presenting It

Show your timeline to your classmates.

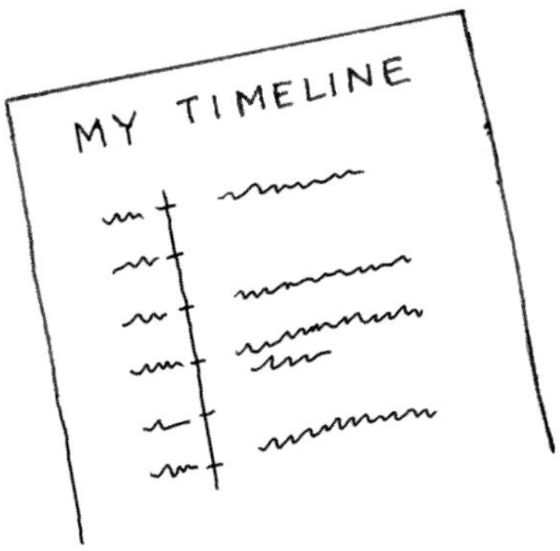

4 I Can Do Things.

A Connecting to Your Life

1 Talk it Over

A. Work with a partner. Look at the pictures. Read the ingredients and actions for making a tuna sandwich.

Ingredients

can of tuna

mayonnaise

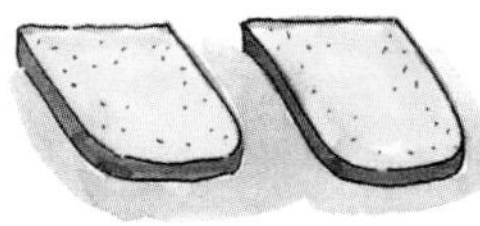

two slices of bread

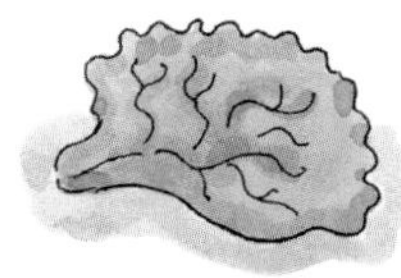

lettuce leaf

Actions

open

mix

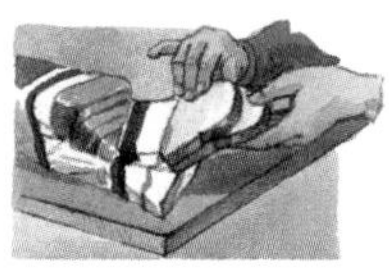

take

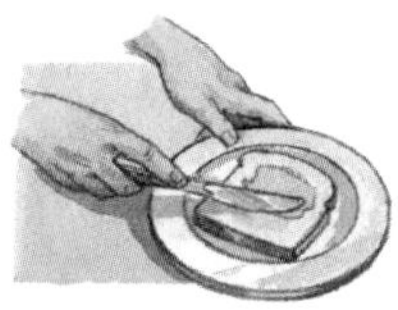

spread

place

B. Make a sandwich. Put the sentences in the right order. Write 1–5 on the lines.

_____ a. Place the lettuce on the tuna.

__1__ b. Open a can of tuna.

_____ c. Spread the tuna on one slice of bread.

_____ d. Take out two slices of bread.

_____ e. Mix the tuna with mayonnaise.

2 Do It

A. Think of things you do that have steps. Make a list.

making a sandwich ____________________ ____________________

____________________ ____________________

____________________ ____________________

B. Share your list with a partner. Circle one thing on your list that is not on your partner's list.

C. Look at the pictures. Complete the missing step.

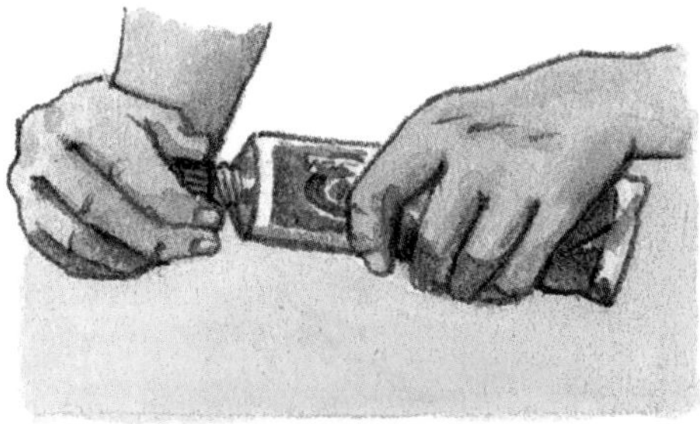

1. Open the toothpaste.

2. Put ____________________ on your toothbrush.

3. Brush your teeth.

4. Spit out the toothpaste.

B Reading

1 Let's Read A flow diagram shows the steps in a process. Read a flow diagram that shows how bread is made.

A farmer grows and harvests wheat.

↓

A truck takes the wheat to a mill.

↓

The mill turns the wheat into flour.

↓

A baker makes dough with the flour.

↗

The baker divides the dough into loaves.

↓

The baker puts the loaves in the oven.

↓

The baker slices each loaf and puts it in a bag.

↓

A truck takes the bread to the grocery store.

2 Unlock Meaning Put the steps in the correct order. Write the numbers 1–6 on the lines.

_____ a. A mill makes flour.

_____ b. The baker cuts the dough into loaves.

_____ c. A baker makes dough.

__1__ d. A farmer harvests wheat.

_____ e. The baker bakes the bread.

_____ f. The baker puts the bread in a bag.

3 Build Fluency Listen to each sentence. Repeat.

1. A farmer grows wheat.
2. A truck takes the wheat to a mill.
3. The mill makes flour.
4. A baker makes dough.
5. The baker divides the dough into loaves.
6. The baker bakes the loaves in the oven.
7. The baker slices each loaf and puts it in a bag.
8. A truck takes the bread to the market.

4 Talk about It

A. Work with a partner. How do you make toast? Draw pictures here.

C Phonics

1 See It, Say It
Listen to each pair of words. Say each word aloud.

loaf

loaves

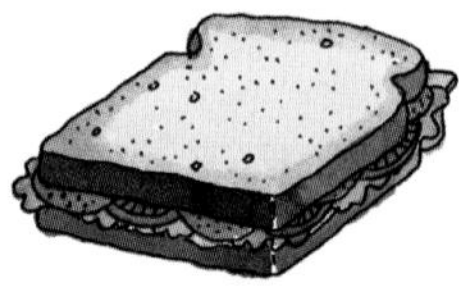
sandwich

sandwiches

can

cans

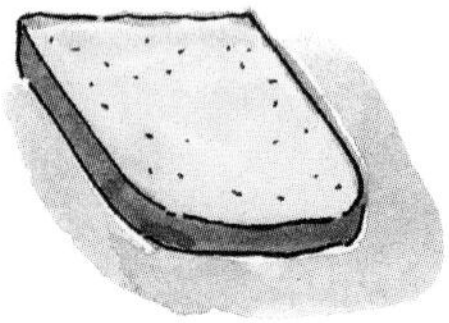
slice

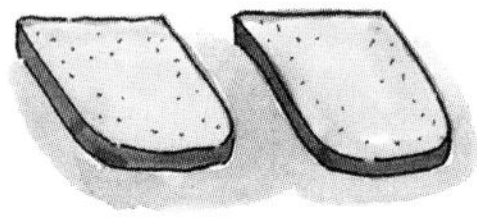
slices

2 Learn the Rule

Most nouns are made plural by adding an -s:

dog – dogs   window – windows   door – doors   cuff – cuffs

When a noun ends in the sounds /s/, /z/, /j/, /sh/, /ch/, or /x/, the plural form is -es. It sounds like /ĭ/ /z/.

dress – dresses   dish – dishes   inch – inches   box – boxes

Some nouns that end in -f or -fe have a plural form -ves. It sounds like /v/ /z/.

knife – knives   loaf – loaves

3 Fun with Words
Complete each sentence. Write the plural form.

1. Juan ate two sandwiches. (sandwich)
2. Cats have nine ______________. (life)
3. I wash the ______________ after dinner. (dish)
4. Lori gave her mother ______________. (rose)
5. The tree is shedding its ______________. (leaf)
6. Tran is taking six ______________. (class)

D Grammar

1 Talk to Others Listen to the dialog. Act it out.

Juan: Who makes dinner at your house?

Lori: My mom **does**. She **makes** dinner. She **likes** to cook.

Juan: Who sets the table?

Lori: I **set** the table.

Juan: Who washes the dishes?

Lori: My mom and dad. They both **wash** the dishes.

2 Learn the Rule

When the subject of the sentence is singular, add an -s to most verbs:

A farmer **grows** wheat.

When the subject is plural or *I* or *you*, use the regular form of the verb:

Farmers **grow** wheat.

PRESENT TENSE AFFIRMATIVE STATEMENTS		
I We You They	**eat**	dinner.
He She It	**eats**	

3 Practice Read each sentence. Circle the correct verb form.

1. Juan (eat/eats) breakfast every morning.
2. Teenagers (need/needs) a healthy breakfast.
3. My teacher (like/likes) her students.
4. Teachers (give/gives) tests.
5. Cows (eat/eats) grass.

E Content Connections

1 Let's Read Flow diagrams can help you learn about our world. This flow diagram describes the life cycle of a butterfly.

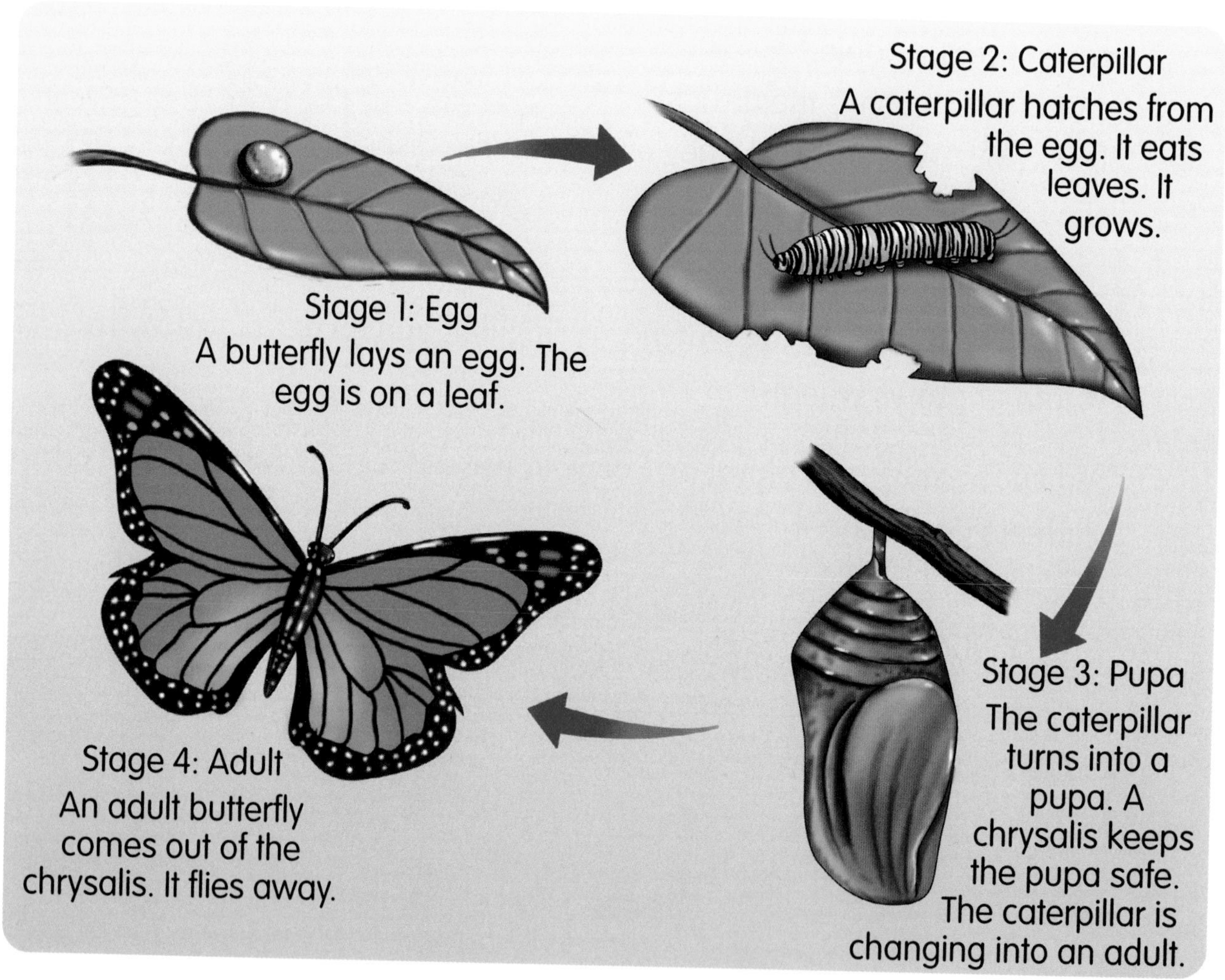

Stage 2: Caterpillar
A caterpillar hatches from the egg. It eats leaves. It grows.
Stage 1: Egg
A butterfly lays an egg. The egg is on a leaf.
Stage 3: Pupa
The caterpillar turns into a pupa. A chrysalis keeps the pupa safe. The caterpillar is changing into an adult.
Stage 4: Adult
An adult butterfly comes out of the chrysalis. It flies away.

2 On Your Own Look at the picture of the monarch butterfly. Write one or two sentences about the butterfly. Use the words below.

beautiful	orange	wings
legs	black	tiny

____

____

3 Think about It Work with a partner. Read the sentences about the life cycle of a frog. Label the flow diagram.

a. The tadpole grows into a baby **frog with a tail**.

b. A frog lays tiny **eggs** in the water.

c. A **tadpole** hatches from an egg.

d. The baby frog grows into an **adult frog**. It loses its tail.

e. The tadpole grows tiny legs.

F Writing

Make a flow diagram.

1 Getting It Out Look at your list in Activity 2A on page 105. Choose something that has at least five steps.

2 Getting It Down Draft your flow diagram.

A. Sketch each step. Use pencil.

B. Write a sentence that describes each step.

C. Add arrows to your diagram.

3 Getting It Right

A. Show your flow diagram to your neighbor.

B. Make changes or corrections.

C. Finish your flow diagram. Use pen.

4 Presenting It

Show your flow diagram to your classmates.

5 Let's Find Out.

A Connecting to Your Life

1 Talk it Over

A. Ask a friend when he or she was born.

When were you born?
I was born on January 1, 1993.

B. Find others who were born in the same month as you. Form a group.

2 Do It

A. Help your teacher record the number of students in your class born in each month.

a. January __________

b. February __________

c. March __________

d. April __________

e. May __________

f. June __________

g. July __________

h. August __________

i. September __________

j. October __________

k. November __________

l. December __________

B. Circle the three months with the most birthdays.

C. Make a column graph for the top three months. Fill in one cell for each person in each month.

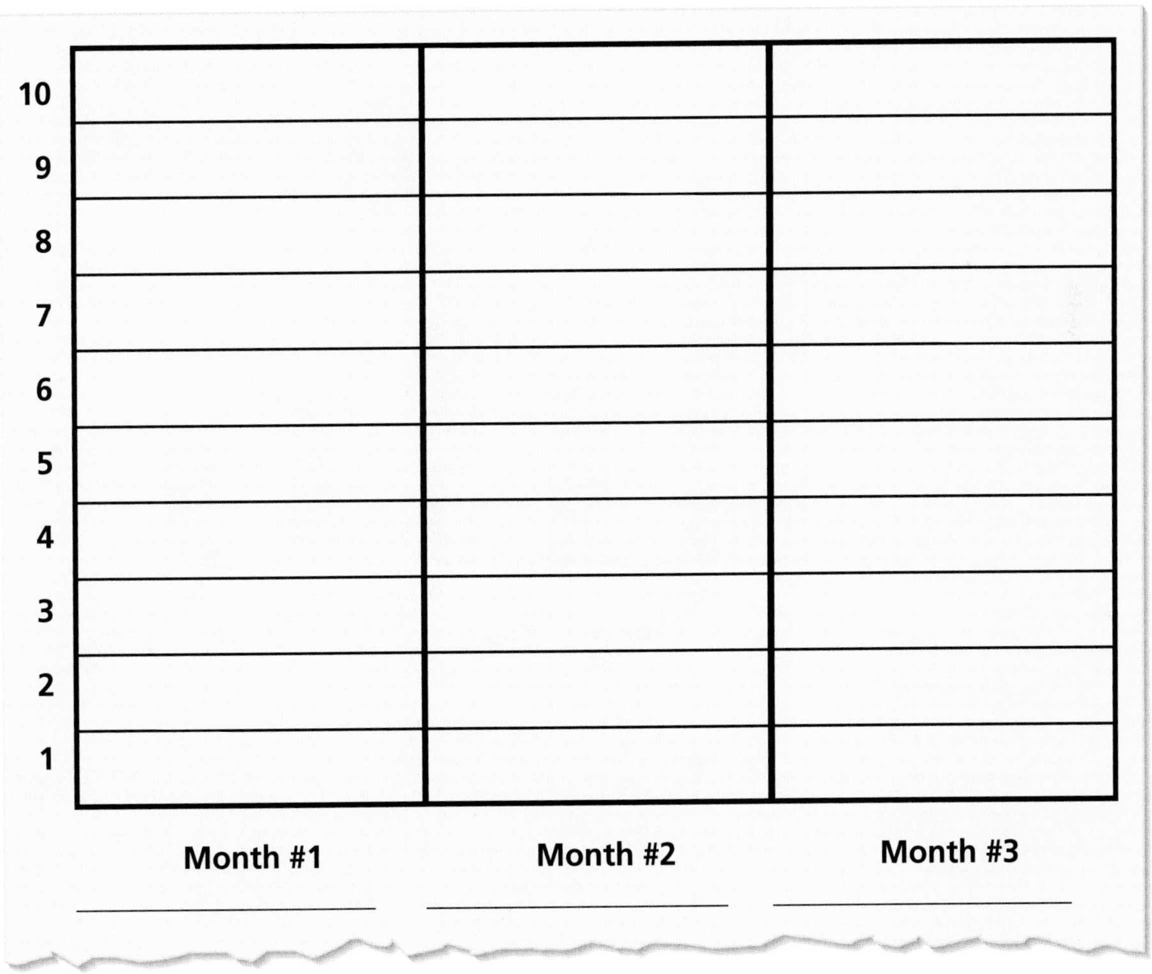

B Reading

1 Let's Read Juan asked 100 classmates to name their favorite team sport. Here is what they said.

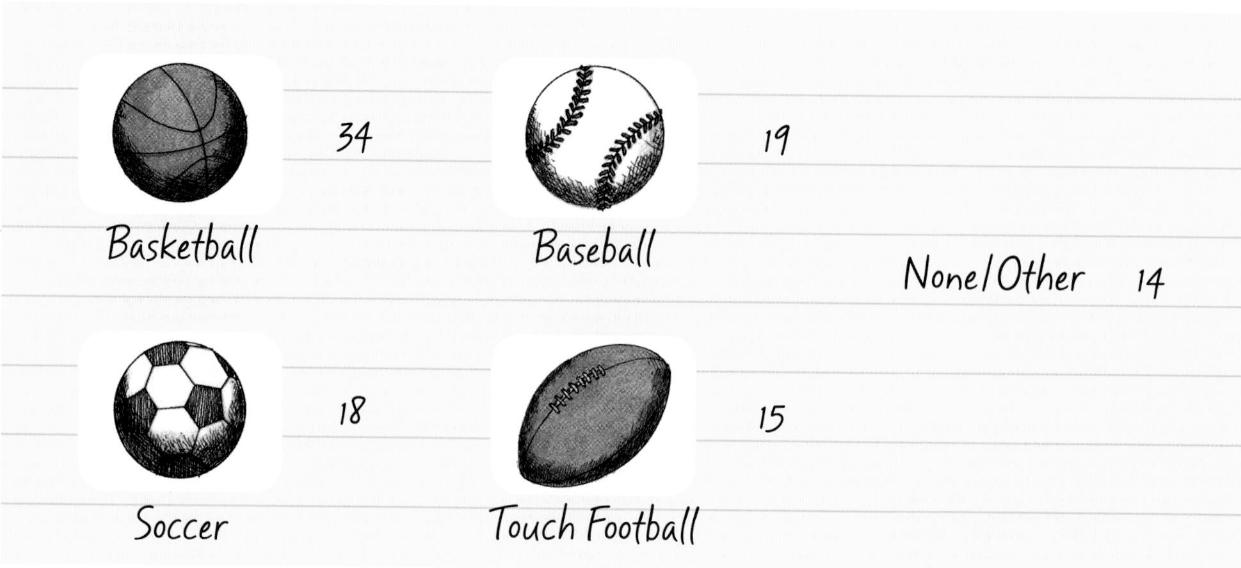

Juan made a column graph to show the results. Read the chart.

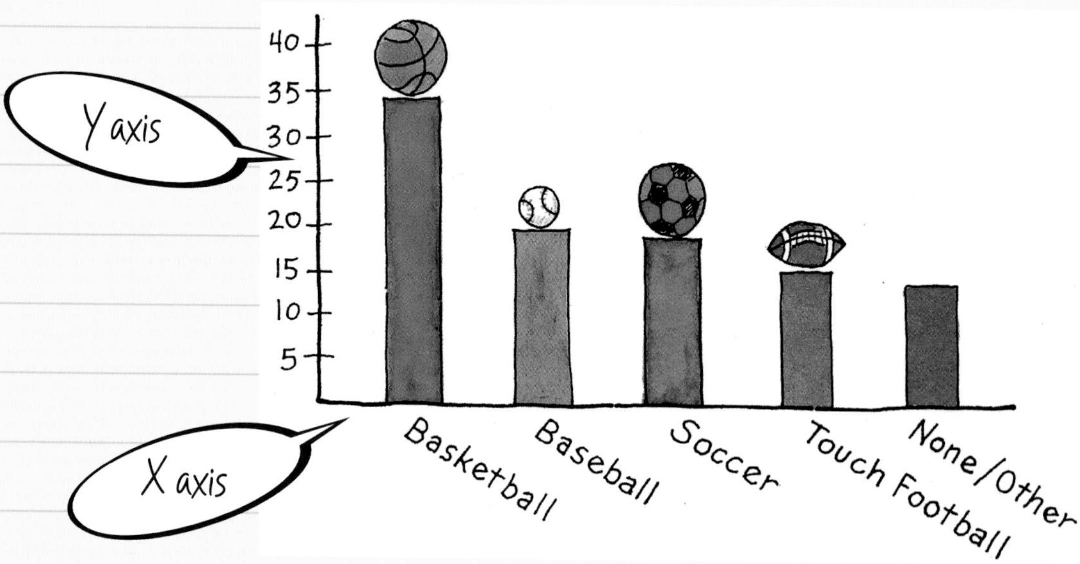

Most people like sports. The most popular team sport is basketball. Baseball and soccer are also popular. The least popular team sport is touch football.

2 Unlock Meaning Read each sentence. Look at Juan's column graph. Write *T* on the line if it is true. Write *F* on the line if it is false.

__F__ 1. All people like sports.

_____ 2. More people like basketball than any other sport.

_____ 3. Baseball is not popular.

_____ 4. Touch football is the least popular sport.

_____ 5. More people like football than soccer.

3 Build Fluency Listen. Work with a partner. Read the dialog.

Question: Do you like soccer?
Answer: Yes, I do. I like soccer.
Question: Do you like volleyball?
Answer: No, I don't. I don't like volleyball.
Question: Do you like baseball?
Answer: Yes, I do. I like baseball.
Question: Do you like football?
Answer: No, I don't. I don't like football.
Question: Do you like basketball?
Answer: I love basketball! It's my favorite sport!

don't = do not

4 Talk about It Many people like individual sports. Check (✓) the sport you like most. Share with a partner.

_____ 1. swimming

_____ 2. running

_____ 3. in-line skating

_____ 4. skateboarding

_____ 5. martial arts

_____ 6. biking

_____ 7. ____________________

martial arts

C Phonics

1 See It, Say It Listen to each word. Pay attention to the sound of the vowel highlighted in yellow. Say each word aloud.

principal pencil favorite August

2 Learn the Rule

When a word has two or more syllables, one syllable is *stressed*. The other syllables are *unstressed*.

SOCcer PRINcipal FAvorite

When a syllable is unstressed, the vowel often sounds like /ə/.

banana holiday second stadium

3 Fun with Words Work with a partner. Read the words aloud. Listen. Circle the vowels that sound like /ə/.

1. America
2. breakfast
3. stomach
4. chicken
5. biology
6. China
7. calendar
8. eleven
9. period
10. April

D Grammar

1 Talk to Others Listen to the dialog. Act it out.

Juan: Do you like soccer?

Lori: Yes, I do. I like soccer.

Juan: Do you like volleyball?

Lori: No, I **don't**. I **don't** like volleyball.

Juan: Does Maria like baseball?

Lori: Yes, she does. She likes baseball a lot.

Juan: What about Tran? Does he like baseball?

Lori: No, he **doesn't** like baseball. He likes football.

2 Learn the Rule Make a present tense sentence negative by adding *do/does + not* before the verb. People often use contractions (*don't, doesn't*), especially when they speak.

PRESENT TENSE NEGATIVE STATEMENTS		
I We You They	**do not/don't**	like soccer.
He She It	**does not/doesn't**	like soccer.

3 Practice Complete each sentence. Write *do not* or *does not*.

1. Juan likes baseball. He __does not__ like volleyball.
2. I like mushroom pizza. I ____________ like pepperoni pizza.
3. Tran and his brother like math. They ____________ like science.
4. Maria likes hip hop. She ____________ like rock and roll.
5. Sam and I both like to watch TV. We ____________ like to do homework.

E Content Connections

1 Let's Read

A. Practice reading large numbers. Listen and repeat.

1	one
10	ten
100	one hundred
1,000	one thousand
10,000	ten thousand
100,000	one hundred thousand
1,000,000	one million
10,000,000	ten million

B. Graphs show numbers or amounts of things. Read this column graph.

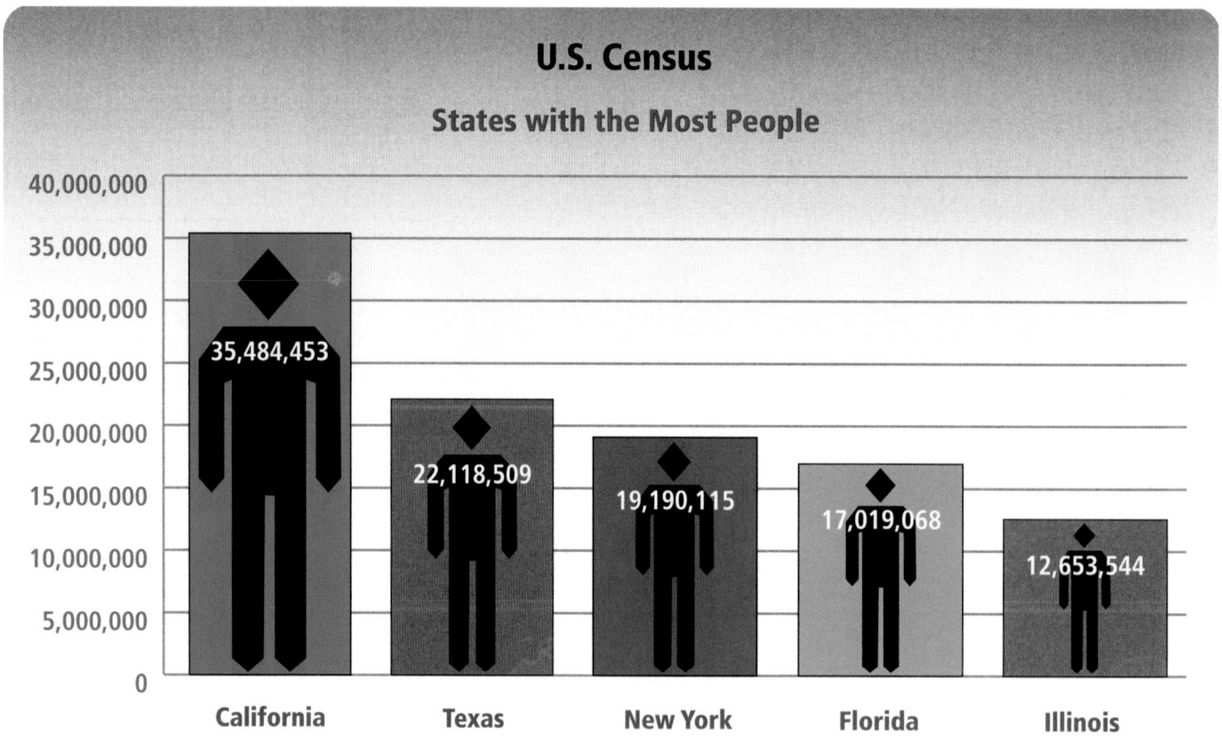

California has the most people. It has more people than the other states. Texas has more people than New York. It has fewer people than California.

2 On Your Own Read the graph on page 120. Complete each sentence. Use the words below.

the most	more	fewer

1. California has _the most_ people.
2. Texas has ____________ people than New York.
3. New York has ____________ people than Florida.
4. Florida has ____________ people than Texas.
5. Florida has ____________ people than Illinois.

3 Think about It Line graphs show changes in numbers. What does this line graph say? Talk it over.

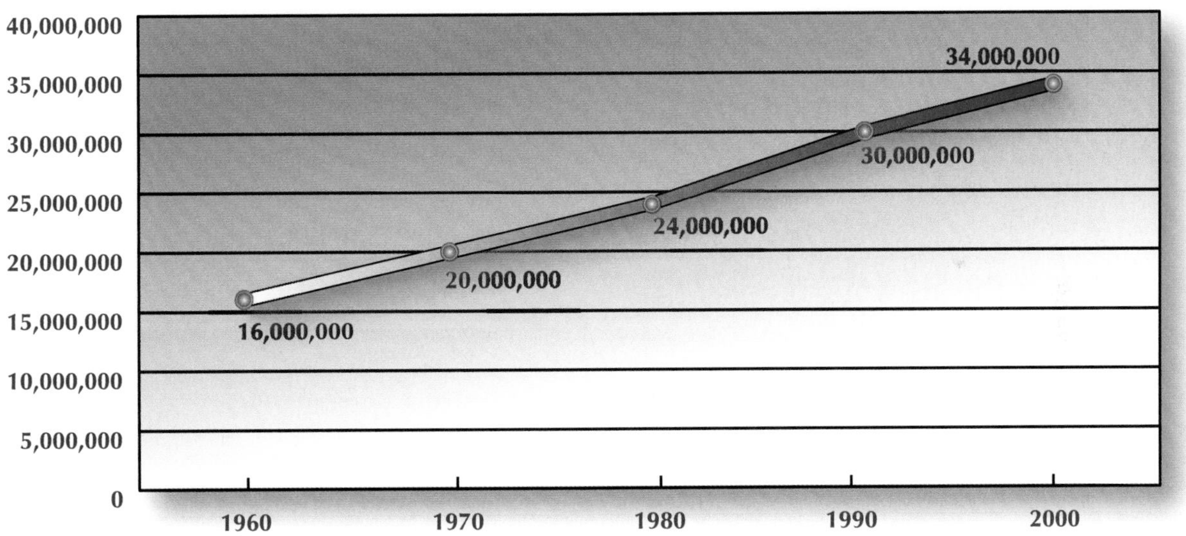

Number of People in California

F Writing

Make a column graph. Interview your classmates.

1 Getting It Out

A. Choose a question to ask.

What is your favorite ____________?

B. Ask ten people. Write down their answers on a separate sheet of paper.

2 Getting It Down

Make a column graph on a separate sheet of paper. Use pencil.

A. Make ruled grid lines.

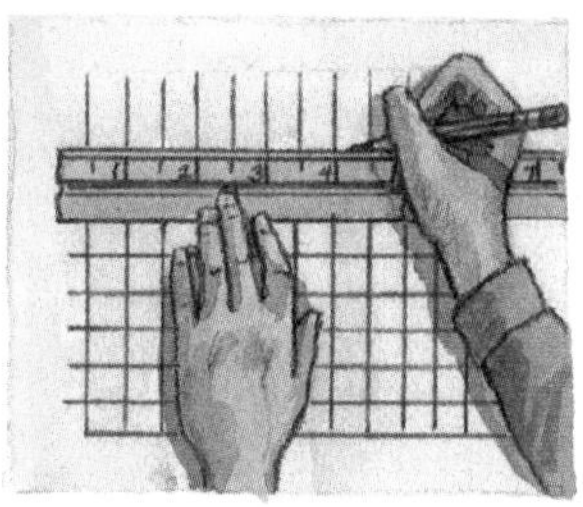

B. Write 1–10 along the Y-axis.

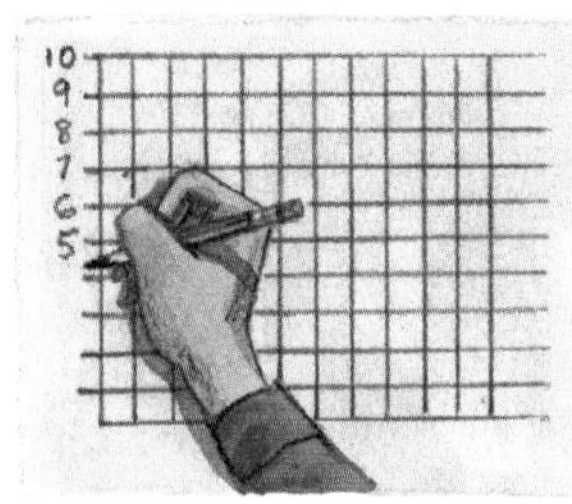

C. Write the answers people give along the X-axis.

D. Fill in a square for each person.

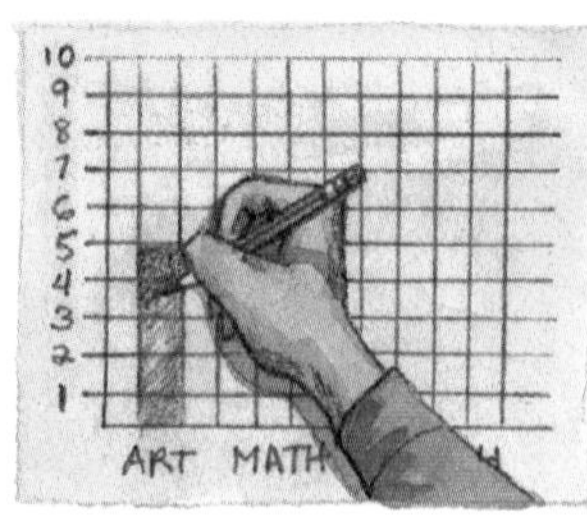

E. Give your graph a title. Write two or three sentences about the information in your graph.

3 Getting It Right

A. Show your column graph to your neighbor.

B. Make changes or corrections.

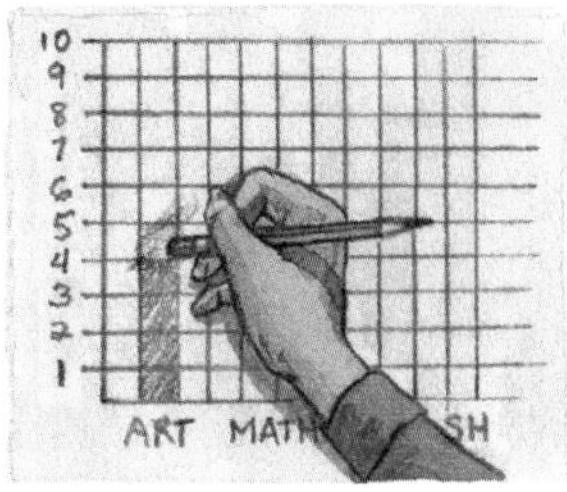

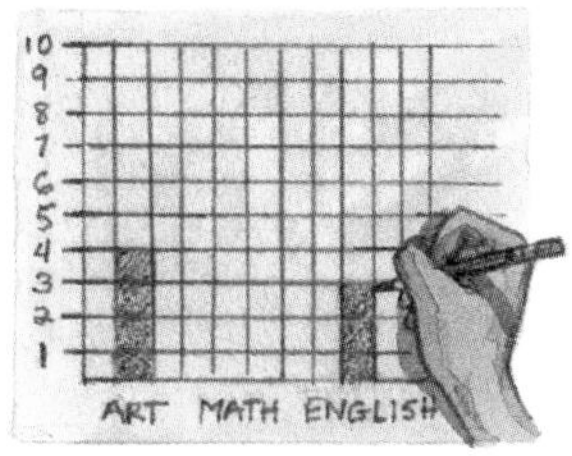

C. Finish your column graph. Use pens and markers.

4 Presenting It

Show your column graph to your classmates.

6 Big, Tall, and Wide

A Connecting to Your Life

1 Talk It Over

A. Work with a partner. Choose three objects in your classroom. Write the objects in the chart below.

B. Estimate the dimensions of each object. Write the dimensions in the chart.

Objects	Estimates (Guesses)		
	Tall/High	Wide	Deep
Bookcase	6 feet high	3 feet wide	14 inches
1.			
2.			
3.			

❷ Do It

A. With your partner, check your estimates. Measure each object. Write each dimension.

Objects	Actual Measurements		
	Tall/High	Wide	Deep
1.			
2.			
3.			

B. Choose <u>one object</u> that is tall, wide, and deep. Make a drawing that shows each side.

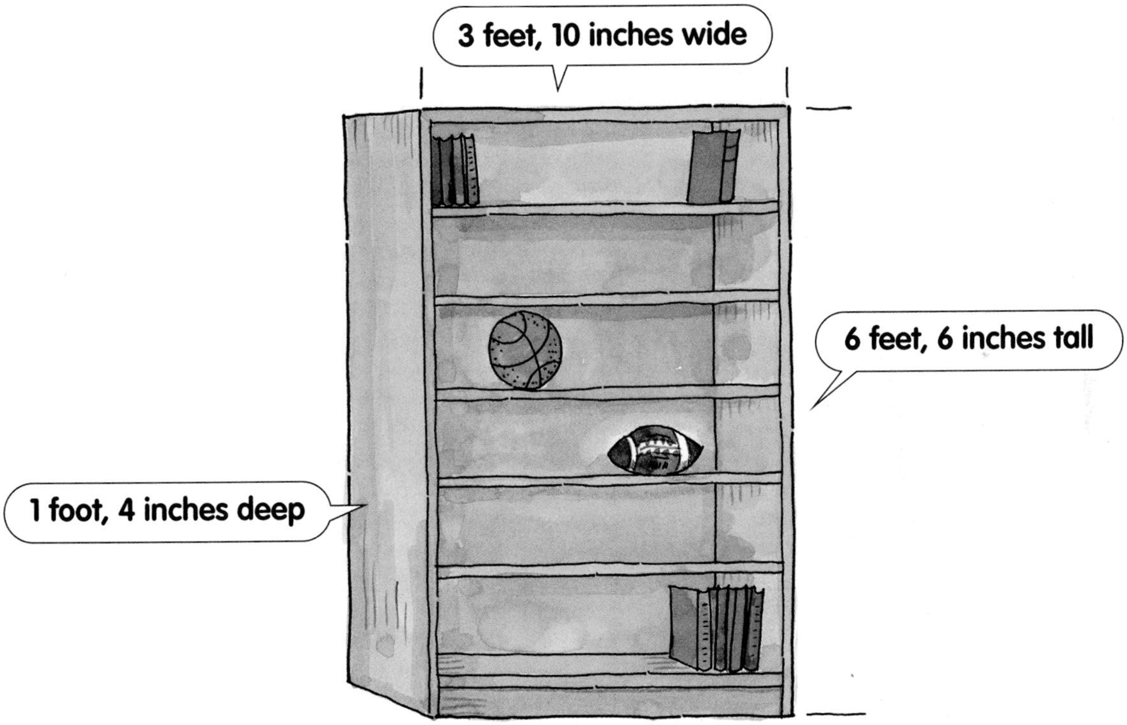

C. Complete the sentence about one of the objects that you measured. Use measurement terms.

The __________________ is __________________ tall/high,
__________________ wide, and __________________ deep.

B Reading

1 Let's Read Lori's family loves pets. They have three dogs. Lori made a scale diagram that compares their sizes. Read the diagram.

Scale: ½ inch = 5 inches

Our family has three dogs. Chico is a chihuahua. He is tiny. Chipper is a corgi. He has short legs and a long body. He is medium-sized. Colette is a collie. She is a large dog.

2 Unlock Meaning

Read each sentence. Write *T* if it is true. Write *F* if it is false.

T 1. Chico is a small dog.

_____ 2. Chipper is very tall.

_____ 3. Colette is two feet tall.

_____ 4. Chico is a foot tall.

_____ 5. Colette is big.

_____ 6. Chipper is two feet long.

3 Build Fluency

Listen. Work with a partner. Read the dialog.

Juan: Do you have any pets?

Lori: We have three dogs.

Juan: What are their names?

Lori: Chico, Chipper, and Colette.

4 Talk about It

A. Draw an animal. Draw a side view. Estimate (guess) its size.

Scale: ½ inch = 5 inches

B. Describe the animal. Write two to three sentences.

C Phonics

1 See It, Say It Listen to each word. Say each word aloud.

cat

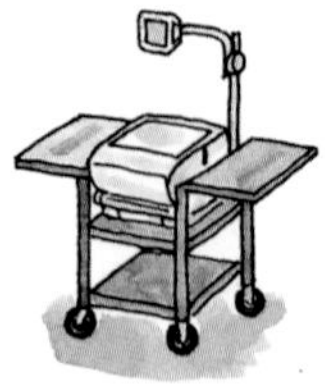
cart

gem

germ

hut

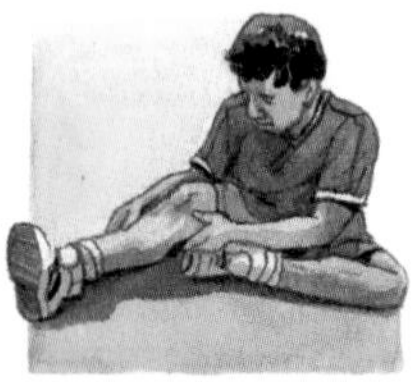
hurt

spot

sport

2 Learn the Rule When a vowel is followed by **r**, it changes its sound—

When **a** is followed by **r**, it often sounds like the *a* in car
When **e**, **i**, and **u** are followed by **r**, they often sound like the *e* in germ.
When **o** is followed by **r**, it often sounds like the *o* in sport.

3 Fun with Words Listen to each word. Write the word in the correct column.

Sounds like **car**	Sounds like **germ**	Sounds like **sport**

1. herd

2. farm

3. shorts

4. purse

$\frac{1}{3}$
5. one-third

D Grammar

1 Talk to Others Listen to the dialog. Act it out.

Juan: Tell me about Chipper.

Lori: He has short legs. His body **is long**.

Juan: What about Colette?

Lori: She has long legs. She **is tall**.

Juan: Are they good dogs?

Lori: Yes, they are. All three **are nice** and **friendly**.

2 Learn the Rule

Use the verb *be* with an adjective to describe a noun.

PRESENT TENSE OF BE + ADJECTIVE		
	BE	**Adjective**
I	**am**	**tall.**
We You They	**are**	**tall.**
He She It	**is**	**tall.**

3 Practice Make eight sentences using *is* or *are* and the words below. Use a separate piece of paper. Add other nouns and adjectives.

Adjectives

long	tall	round	________	________
small	square	big	________	________

Nouns

trains	the earth	a bee	an eel	________
gorillas	some boxes	basketballs	dinosaurs	________

E Content connections

1 Let's Read Scientists use scale diagrams. Learn about dinosaurs. Practice sounding out each name.

Scale: ½ inch = 6 feet

Brachiosaurus	75 feet long	40 feet tall	
Iguanodon	33 feet long	20 feet tall	
Pterodactyl	25 feet from wing-tip to wing-tip		
Tyrannosaurus	50 feet long	20 feet tall	7 inch teeth

Dinosaurs lived many millions of years ago. They were reptiles. Some, like the brachiosaurus and the iguanodon, ate plants. Others, like the tyrannosaurus, ate meat—mostly other dinosaurs!

2 On Your Own Choose one dinosaur. Write three sentences about it on a piece of paper.

3 Think about It

A. This scale diagram shows the size of the planets. Read the information aloud.

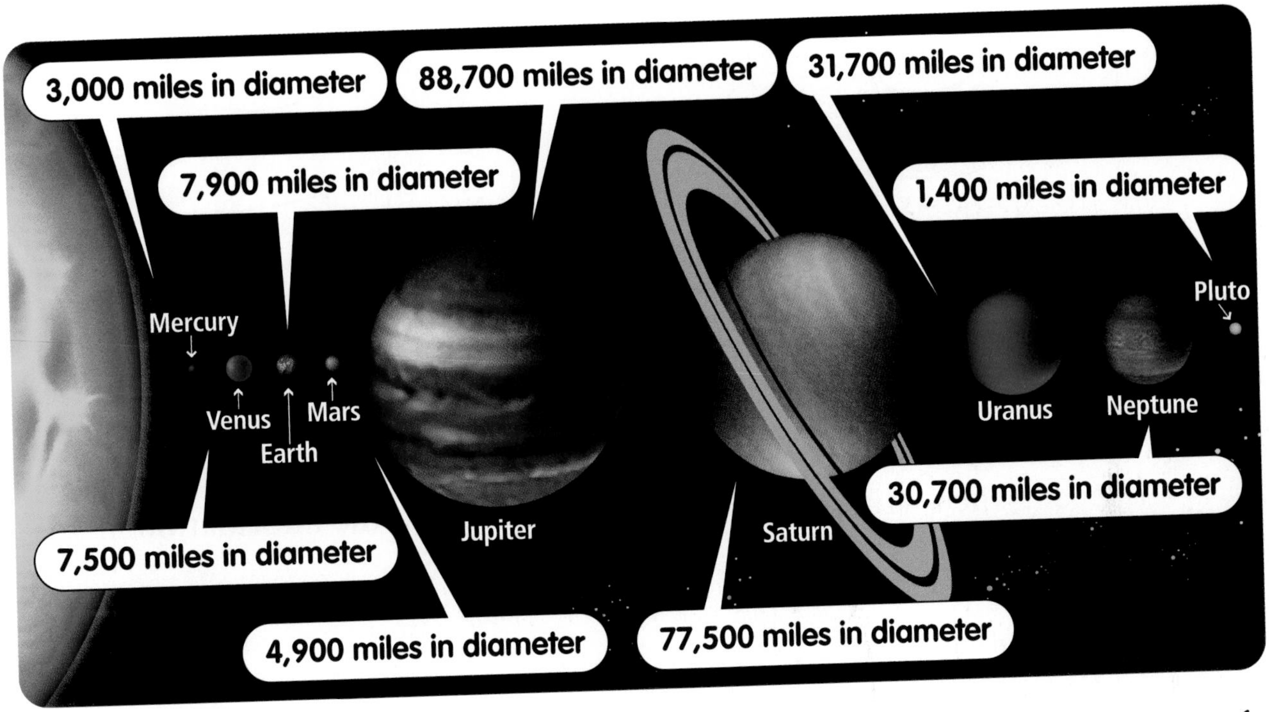

B. Work with a partner. Think of everyday objects to compare with the size of the planets. Complete the chart.

Planet	Object
Mercury	grain of rice
Venus	
Earth	pea
Mars	
Jupiter	grapefruit
Saturn	baseball
Uranus	
Neptune	golf ball
Pluto	

F Writing

Make a scale diagram for objects in your classroom.

1 Getting It Out Choose two objects to compare. Sketch each object on a separate sheet of paper. Take measurements.

my shoe

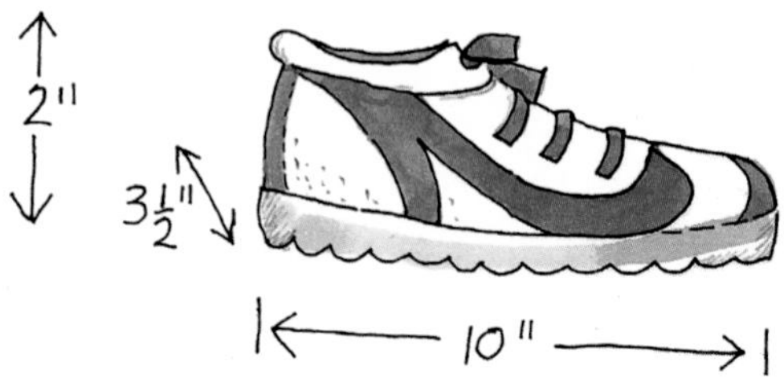

my friend's shoe

2 Getting It Down Draft your drawing. Decide on the scale. Use a pencil. Then write two to three sentences about the information in your diagram.

Scale: ½ inch = _____

3 Getting It Right

A. Measure each object one more time.

B. Make corrections and add labels.

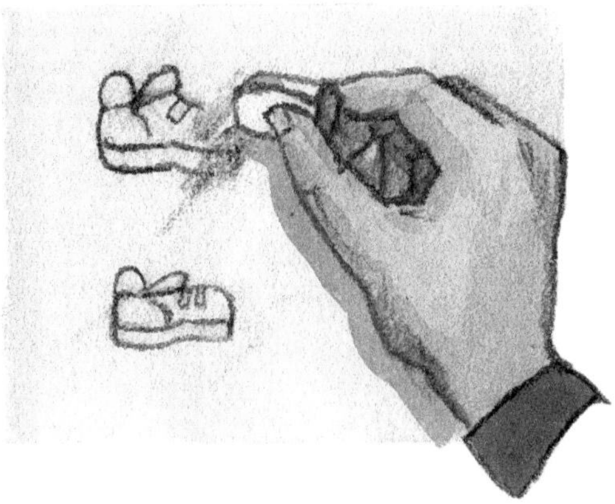

C. Finish your drawing. Use a pen.

4 Presenting It

Show your scale diagram to your classmates. Describe it.

This is my shoe, and this is Carlos's shoe. My shoe is 12 $\frac{1}{2}$ inches long. Carlos's shoe is 10 inches long.

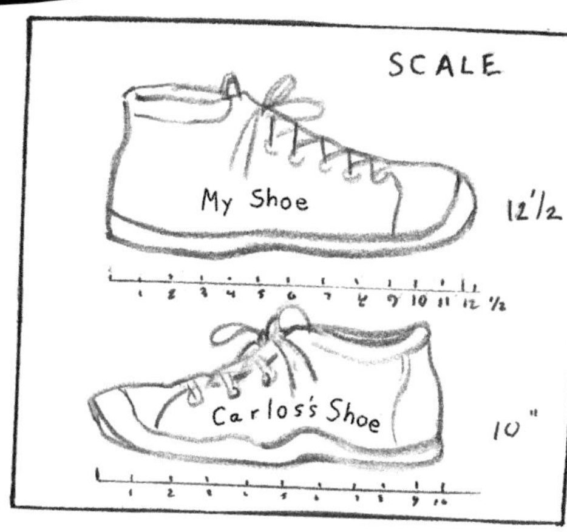

ChecBrics*

UNIT 1

ChecBric for Venn Diagram

Focus	Overall rating
Content & Organization ____ My diagram compares the TV shows I like and the TV shows my partner likes. ____ I include three sentences about my diagram. ____ The information is correct.	____ 4 = Wow! ____ 3 = Good ____ 2 = OK ____ 1 = Needs work
Language & Conventions ____ I use complete sentences. ____ I use correct pronouns. ____ I spell words correctly.	____ 4 = Wow! ____ 3 = Good ____ 2 = OK ____ 1 = Needs work

UNIT 2

ChecBric for Family Tree

Focus	Overall rating
Content & Organization ____ My family tree shows everyone in my family. ____ I include three sentences about my family. ____ The information is correct.	____ 4 = Wow! ____ 3 = Good ____ 2 = OK ____ 1 = Needs work
Language & Conventions ____ I use complete sentences. ____ I use correct possessive adjectives. ____ I capitalize the names of my family members correctly.	____ 4 = Wow! ____ 3 = Good ____ 2 = OK ____ 1 = Needs work

**ChecBric name and concept created by Larry Lewin.*

UNIT 3

ChecBric for Personal Timeline

Focus	Overall rating
Content & Organization ____ My timeline shows important events in my life. ____ I include five sentences about my life. ____ I include a picture showing one event.	____ 4 = Wow! ____ 3 = Good ____ 2 = OK ____ 1 = Needs work
Language & Conventions ____ I use sentences with nouns and verbs. ____ I spell words correctly.	____ 4 = Wow! ____ 3 = Good ____ 2 = OK ____ 1 = Needs work

UNIT 4

ChecBric for Flow Diagram

Focus	Overall rating
Content & Organization ____ My flow diagram shows steps in a process. ____ The steps are in the correct order. ____ The information is correct.	____ 4 = Wow! ____ 3 = Good ____ 2 = OK ____ 1 = Needs work
Language & Conventions ____ I use complete sentences. ____ I use correct grammar. ____ I spell words correctly.	____ 4 = Wow! ____ 3 = Good ____ 2 = OK ____ 1 = Needs work

UNIT 5

ChecBric for Column Graph

Focus	Overall rating
Content & Organization ____ My column graph presents information about my classmates' favorite things ____ I label each axis correctly. ____ The information in each column is accurate. ____ I include two or three sentences about the information in my graph.	____ 4 = Wow! ____ 3 = Good ____ 2 = OK ____ 1 = Needs work
Language & Conventions ____ I use complete sentences. ____ I use correct grammar. ____ I spell words correctly.	____ 4 = Wow! ____ 3 = Good ____ 2 = OK ____ 1 = Needs work

UNIT 6

ChecBric for Scale Diagram

Focus	Overall rating
Content & Organization ____ My scale diagram compares two objects. ____ My drawings are to scale. ____ The labeling is correct. ____ I include two or three sentences about the objects.	____ 4 = Wow! ____ 3 = Good ____ 2 = OK ____ 1 = Needs work
Language & Conventions ____ I use complete sentences. ____ I use the correct form of *be*. ____ I spell words correctly.	____ 4 = Wow! ____ 3 = Good ____ 2 = OK ____ 1 = Needs work

Listening Script

SECTION A, UNIT 1

1. B. Listen and Repeat (page 4)

A, B, C, D
E, F, G
H, I, J, K
L, M, N, O, P
Q, R, S, T
U and V
W
X
Y
and Z!

SECTION A, UNIT 2

2. Thumbs Up, Thumbs Down (page 7)

a. three
b. nine
c. fourteen
d. thirteen
e. fifty-eight

SECTION A, UNIT 3

1. A. Listen and Repeat (page 8)

Sunday, Monday, Tuesday, Wednesday,
Thursday, Friday, Saturday

1. B.

September first
September second
September third
September fourth
September fifth
September sixth
September seventh
September eighth
September ninth
September tenth
September eleventh
September twelfth
September thirteenth
September fourteenth
September fifteenth
September sixteenth
September seventeenth
September eighteenth
September nineteenth
September twentieth
September twenty-first
September twenty-second
September twenty-third
September twenty-fourth
September twenty-fifth
September twenty-sixth
September twenty-seventh
September twenty-eighth
September twenty-ninth
September thirtieth

1. C.

1. January
2. February
3. March
4. April
5. May
6. June
7. July
8. August
9. September
10. October
11. November
12. December

2. Thumbs Up, Thumbs Down (page 8)

1. September sixth
2. December thirtieth
3. May twentieth
4. October tenth
5. February fourth
6. August third

SECTION A, UNIT 4

1. Listen and Repeat (page 10)

Secretary: I'll help you fill out your enrollment form.
Secretary: Today's date is September 7, 2009.
Secretary: What's your last name?
Pablo: Ortiz.
Secretary: What's your first name?
Pablo: Pablo.
Secretary: What's your middle initial?
Pablo: E.
Secretary: What's your address?
Pablo: 123 1st Street, Apartment 43. Oakland, California.
Secretary: What's your ZIP code?
Pablo: 94601.
Secretary: What's your phone number?
Pablo: 510 555-1234.
Secretary: How old are you?
Pablo: 17.
Secretary: Please sign your name. Thank you.

2. Thumbs Up, Thumbs Down (page 10)

1. My first name is Pablo.
2. My last name is Mendez.
3. I live in San Francisco.
4. I live in an apartment.
5. I live in California.
6. I am seven years old.

SECTION A, UNIT 5

1. Listen and Repeat (page 12)

What time is it? It is eight o'clock.
What time is it? It is nine fifteen.
What time is it? It is ten thirty.
What time is it? It is eleven forty-five.
What time is it? It is twelve o'clock. It is noon.
What time is it? It is one twenty.
What time is it? It is two forty.
What time is it? It is three ten.

2. Thumbs Up, Thumbs Down (page 12)

1. two ten
2. six thirty
3. eight forty five
4. nine o'clock
5. ten fourteen
6. noon
7. one thirty
8. two o'clock

SECTION A, UNIT 6

2. Thumbs Up, Thumbs Down (page 16)

1. test, desk
2. time, dime
3. take, tail
4. tub, duck

SECTION A, UNIT 7

2. Thumbs Up, Thumbs Down (page 18)

1. pen, pet
2. bell, pencil
3. pass, pals
4. bus, plus

SECTION A, UNIT 8

2. Thumbs Up, Thumbs Down (page 20)

1. map, nap
2. mail, nail
3. math, man
4. moon, noon

SECTION A, UNIT 9

1. Listen and Repeat (page 22)

1. I live in a city. I live in San Francisco. Find the bridge. Find the tall buildings. Find a park.
2. My city is in a state. I live in California. Find the beach. Find a mountain. Find the lake. Find the river. Find the valley.
3. My state is in a country. I live in the United States. Find the United States. Find Canada. Find Mexico. Find the cities. Find San Francisco. Find Los Angeles. Find Las Vegas. Find Dallas. Find Miami. Find New York. Find Rochester.
4. I live on planet Earth. I come from Laos. I come from Cambodia. I come from China. I come from Japan. I come from Korea. I come from Russia. I come from Lebanon. I come from Romania.

SECTION A, UNIT 10

1. Listen and Repeat (page 24)

1. Hold up your finger.
2. Touch your arm.
3. Touch your back.
4. Touch your elbow.
5. Touch your face.
6. Touch your foot.
7. Touch your hair.
8. Touch your hand.
9. Touch your head.
10. Touch your leg.
11. Touch your shoulder.
12. Touch your thumb.
13. Touch your toe.
14. Touch your knee.

SECTION A, UNIT 11

1. Listen and Repeat (page 26)

Teacher: These are letters.
Consonants: b, c, d, f, g, h, j, k, l, m, n, p, q, r, s, t, v, w, x, y, z.
Vowels: a, e, i, o, u.
These are some words.
Nouns: water, wall, window, vegetables, vacation, video.
Verbs: wake up, wave, walk, visit, vote.
This is a sentence: Vicki is waving to Will.
Homework: Vocabulary words 1–10—Write sentences. Due tomorrow!

2. Thumbs Up, Thumbs Down (page 26)

1. wallet, window
2. water, watch
3. vase, waist
4. volcano, valley

3. Do It (page 27)

1. Circle the letter w.
2. Underline the letter that sounds like /v/.
3. Match the word "volcano" with the picture of a volcano. Match the word "window" with the picture of a window.

SECTION A, UNIT 12

1. Listen and Repeat (page 30)

We have books about yoga, the galaxy, jets, Korea, Jane Goodall, killer whales, gorillas, Japan, and the New York Yankees.

2. Thumbs Up, Thumbs Down (page 30)

1. guy, girl
2. kite, guitar
3. ketchup, kitchen
4. yellow, jelly

SECTION A, UNIT 13

1. Listen and Repeat (page 32)

Boy: In our cafeteria, we have a salad bar. There are carrots ... lettuce ... tomatoes ... cucumbers ... and celery.

Girl: We have sandwiches. There are submarine sandwiches ... tuna sandwiches ... and turkey sandwiches.

Boy: We have specials. There is chicken soup and there is macaroni and cheese.

Girl: We have drinks. There is milk. There is water. And there is juice.

Boy: We have desserts. There is cake. There are cinnamon cookies. There is low-fat yogurt. And there is fruit.

SECTION A, UNIT 14

1. Listen and Repeat (page 34)

I see gold.
I see red.
I see brown.
I see white.
I see silver.
I see cream.
I see green.
I see black.
I see purple.
I see yellow.
I see blue.
I see pink.
I see orange.
I see gray.
I see a line.
I see a circle.
I see a square.
I see a rectangle.
I see a triangle.

2. Thumbs Up, Thumbs Down (page 34)

1. crab, clap
2. brain, bleed
3. fruit, flower
4. grin, grandfather

SECTION A, UNIT 15

1. Listen and Repeat (page 36)

I see plants. I see a tree. I see a flower. I see a shrub or bush. I see grass.

I see animals. I see fish. I see a shark. I see a shellfish.

I see birds. I see a parrot. I see a duck.

I see mammals. I see a chimpanzee. I see a panther.

I see insects. I see a cockroach. I see a bee.

SECTION A, UNIT 16

1. Listen and Repeat (page 40)

What to you like to do after school?
I like to play squash.
I like to skateboard.
I like to play sports.
I like to ride my scooter.
I like to study.
I like to have a snack.
I like to read a story.

2. Thumbs Up, Thumbs Down (page 40)

1. skull, student
2. smell, scream
3. spaghetti, skeleton
4. sneeze, smile

SECTION B, UNIT 1

3. Listen and Read (page 43)

1. rat
2. cat
3. man
4. bag
5. pass
6. Jan

SECTION B, UNIT 2

3. Listen and Read (page 47)

1. bed
2. man
3. pan
4. send
5. pet
6. Tad

SECTION B, UNIT 3

3. Listen and Read (page 51)

1. thank
2. blink
3. hit
4. ten
5. pen
6. spill

SECTION B, UNIT 4

3. Listen and Read (page 55)

1. nut
2. dock
3. rub
4. cot
5. sock
6. hut

SECTION B, UNIT 5

3. Listen and Read (page 59)

1. pail
2. back
3. Jan
4. snake
5. pan
6. paints

SECTION B, UNIT 6

3. Listen and Read (page 63)

1. shape
2. week
3. Jean
4. seal
5. mail
6. feel

SECTION B, UNIT 7

3. Listen and Read (page 67)

1. seed
2. bee
3. wide
4. bite
5. feet
6. time

Index

Grammar and Mechanics

Listening and Speaking

Phonics and Spelling

Reading and Writing Genres

Reading (Comprehension strategies, skills, text organization)

Real World Applications

Visual Literacy

Vocabulary

Writing

Photo Credits

Cover Images: (top left): © Creatas/PunchStock; (top right): © Digital Vision; (middle left): © Dynamic Graphics/JupiterImages; (middle): © StockTrek/Getty Images; (middle right): © Comstock/PictureQuest; (bottom left): © Digital Vision/Getty Images; (bottom middle): © Andersen Ross/Getty Images; (bottom right): © S. Meltzer/PhotoLink/Getty Images.

Interior Images: P. 2: © Digital Vision/SuperStock; 3: © Comstock/PictureQuest; 5 (left to right): © Markus Amon/Getty Images, © Dynamic Graphics/JupiterImages, © Royalty-Free/CORBIS, © Brand X Pictures/PunchStock; 9 (top, left to right): © Blend Images/Alamy, © Chris A Crumley/Alamy, © BananaStock/JupiterImages, © Rim Light/PhotoLink/Getty Images; 9 (bottom, left to right): © Ryan McVay/Getty Images, © SW Productions/Getty Images, © Royalty-Free/CORBIS; 13 (left to right): © Digital Vision/PunchStock, © Steve Hamblin/Alamy, © PhotoDisc/Getty Images, © Image Source/JupiterImages; 14-15 (background): © Christina Kennedy/Getty Images; 14: © Charles Gupton/CORBIS; 15: © Michael Newman/PhotoEdit; 16 (top, left to right): © Ryan McVay/Getty Images, © Image Source/PunchStock; 16 (bottom, left to right): © Randy Allbritton/Getty Images, © Dynamic Graphics Group/Creatas/Alamy, © Getty Images; 17 (left to right): © Image Source/PunchStock, © Blend Images/Alamy, © Chris A Crumley/Alamy, © Corbis/PictureQuest; 18 (top): © Royalty-Free/CORBIS; 18 (bottom, left to right): © Photodics Collection/Getty Images, © PhotoLink/Getty Images, © Royalty-Free/CORBIS; 19 (left to right): © Royalty-Free/CORBIS. © C Squared Studios/Getty Images, © C Squared Studios/Getty Images, © C Squared Studios/Getty Images, © PhotoLink/Getty Images; 20 (top, left to right): © Ryan McVay/Getty Images, © GOODSHOOT/Alamy, Corbis/PictureQuest; 20 (bottom, left to right): © Digital Vision/Getty Images, © Siede Preis/Getty Images, © Royalty-Free/CORBIS; 21 (left to right): © Corbis/PictureQuest, © Royalty-Free/CORBIS; 23 (left to right): © Mel Curtis/Getty Images; © Brand X Pictures/PunchStock; 24 (top left): © image100 Ltd; 24 (top right): © Photodisc/Getty Images; 24 (bottom left): © Barbara Penoyar/Getty Images; 24 (bottom right): The McGraw-Hill Companies, Inc./Eric Wise, photographer; 26 (top, left to right): © PhotoLink/Getty Images, © Ryan McVay/Getty Images, © Jules Frazier/Getty Images, © Rubberball Productions/Getty Images; 26 (bottom, left to right): © Don Farrall/Getty Images, © PhotoDisc/Getty Images, Photo #1 from U.S. Dept of Commerce photoset "Hawaii Volcanism: Lava Forms", © Digital Vision/PunchStock; 27 (top): © Ryan McVay/Getty Images; 27 (middle): Photo #1 from U.S. Dept of Commerce photoset "Hawaii Volcanism: Lava Forms"; 27 (bottom, left to right): © C Squared Studios/Getty Images, © Amos Morgan/Getty Images, © Andersen Ross/Getty Images, Jules Frazier/Getty Images; 28: © Royalty-Free/CORBIS; 29 (top): © Syracuse Newspapers/Stephen Cannerelli/The Image Works; 29 (bottom): © Barros & Barros/Getty Images; 30 (top, left to right): © Royalty-Free/CORBIS, © Ryan McVay/Getty Images, © Photodisc/Getty Images, © Ryan McVay/Getty Images; 30 (bottom, left to right): © Chet Phillips/Getty Images, © C Squared Studios/Getty Images, © John Foxx/Alamy; 31 (left): © PhotoDisc/Getty Images; 31 (right): © Duncan Smith/Getty Images; 33 (left): © C Squared Studios/Getty Images; 33 (right): © SW Productions/Getty Images; 34 (top, left to right): © C Squared Studios/Getty Images, © C Squared Studios/Getty Images, © Andrew Ward/Life File/Getty Images; 34 (bottom right): © Martial Colomb/Getty Images; 35 (left to right): © Brand X Pictures/PunchStock, © PhotoLink/Getty Images, © PhotoLink/Getty Images; 36 (top, left to right): © Royalty-Free/Corbis, © Dave Thompson/Life File/Getty Images, © Royalty-Free/CORBIS, © Creatas/PunchStock; 36 (middle, left to right): © Thinkstock/Getty Images, © C Squared Studios/Getty Images, © G.K. & Vikki Hart/Getty Images, © Getty Images; 36 (bottom, left to right): © Alan and Sandy Carey/Getty Images, © Royalty-Free/CORBIS, © Creatas/PunchStock , © Alan and Sandy Carey/Getty Images; 37 (top, left to right): © Digital Vision, © Creatas/PunchStock, © Brand X Pictures/PunchStock; 37 (second top, left to right): Photo courtesy of USDA Natural Resources Conservation Service, © Brand X Pictures/PunchStock; 37 (second bottom): © Mike Buxton Papilio/CORBIS; 37 (bottom, left to right): © Royalty-Free/CORBIS, © Photodisc/PunchStock, © Ryan McVay/Getty Images, © Photodisc/Getty Images; 38 (top left): © Pierre Burnaugh/PhotoEdit; 38 (top right): © Paul Costello/Getty Images; 38 (middle): © Digital Vision/SuperStock; 38 (bottom): © Leland Bobbe/Getty Images; 39 (top left): © Jeff Greenberg/PhotoEdit; 39 (top right): © Brand X Pictures/Age Fotostock; 39 (middle right): © Photodisc/PunchStock; 39 (bottom left): © Digital Vision/SuperStock; 39 (bottom right): © Ellen Senisi/The Image Works; 40 (top, left to right): The McGraw-Hill Companies, Inc./Photo by Christine Eckel, © Andersen Ross/Getty Images, © C Squared Studios/Getty Images, © Stockbyte/PunchStock; 40 (bottom, left to right): © Andersen Ross/Getty Images, © Brand X Pictures/PunchStock, © Getty Images, © Digital Vision/PunchStock; 41 (left): © Jason Reed/Getty Images; 41 (right): © Andersen Ross/Getty Images; 42 (top, left to right): © Photodisc/PunchStock, © SW Productions/Getty Images, © Comstock/PictureQuest, © Photodisc/PunchStock; 42 (second top, left to right): © BananaStock/PunchStock, © Ryan McVay/Getty Images, © Ryan McVay/Getty Images, © Amos Morgan/Getty Images; 42 (second bottom, left to right): © Ryan McVay/Getty Images, © Barbara Penoyar/Getty Images, © Andersen Ross/Getty Images; 42 (bottom, left to right): © Digital Vision, © Andersen Ross/Getty Images, © Getty Images/Digital Vision; .43 (top to bottom): © Burke/Triolo Productions/Getty Images, © Dynamic Graphics/JupiterImages, The McGraw-Hill Companies, Inc./Eric Wise, photographer, © Creatas/PunchStock; 46 (top to bottom): © Comstock/PictureQuest, © BananaStock/JupiterImages; 47 (top to bottom: © Siede Preis/Getty Images,

© PhotoLink/Getty Images, © Photodics Collection/Getty Images; 48 (top, left to bottom): © Siede Preis/Getty Images, © BananaStock/JupiterImages, © Siede Preis/Getty Images; 48 (bottom, left to right): © Photodisc/Getty Images, Corbis/PictureQuest, © Kim Steele/Getty Images; 50 (left to right): © Dynamic Graphics /JupiterImages, © BananaStock/JupiterImages, © Antonio Mo/Getty Images; 51 (top left): © More/zefa/Corbis; 51 (top right): © SuperStock/Alamy; 51 (middle, top to bottom): The McGraw-Hill Companies, Inc./Jill Braaten, Photographer, © Digital Vision/Getty Images; 54 (top, left to right): © C Squared Studios/Getty Images, © Nick Koudis/Getty Images, © Image Source/PunchStock; 54 (bottom, left to right): © Dinodia Images/Alamy, © Digital Vision/PunchStock, © Brand X Pictures/PunchStock; 55 (top): © Photodisc Collection/Getty Images; 55 (bottom): © John A. Rizzo/Getty Images; 59 (top right): © IT Stock/PunchStock; 59 (middle, top to bottom): © Jules Frazier/Getty Images, © Royalty-Free/CORBIS, © Mel Curtis/Getty Images; 62 (top, left to right); © Alan and Sandy Carey/Getty Images, © Brand X Pictures/PunchStock, © G.K. & Vikki Hart/Getty Images, © Royalty-Free/CORBIS; 62 (second top, left to right): © Digital Vision/Getty Images, © Alan and Sandy Carey/Getty Images, © Geostock/Getty Images, © PhotoLink/Getty Images; 62 (second bottom, left to right): © Royalty-Free/CORBIS, The McGraw-Hill Companies, Inc./John Flournoy, photographer, © Royalty-Free/CORBIS; 62 (bottom, left to right); © Stockdisc/PunchStock, © Image Source/JupiterImages, © C Squared Studios/Getty Images; 63 (top to bottom): © Image Source/JupiterImages, © Royalty-Free/CORBIS, © Royalty-Free/CORBIS; 64 (top, left to right): © Alan and Sandy Carey/Getty Images, © PhotoLink/Getty Images, © G.K. & Vikki Hart/Getty Images; 64 (second top, left to right): © Digital Vision/Getty Images, © Stockbyte, © Brand X Pictures/PunchStock; 64 (second bottom, right): © Photodisc/Getty Images; 64 (bottom left); © Digital Vision/Getty Images; 64 (bottom right): © C Squared Studios/Getty Images; 66 (left): © Randy Allbritton/Getty Images; 66 (right): © Jules Frazier/Getty Images; 67 (top left): © Mark Sykes/Alamy; 67 (top right): © Image Source/Alamy; 67 (middle, top to bottom): © C Squared Studios/Getty Images, © Randy Allbritton/Getty Images; 71 (top, left to right); © Jules Frazier/Getty Images, © Adrian Weinbrecht/Getty Images, © C Squared Studios/Getty Images; 71 (bottom, left to right): © Photodisc/Getty Images, © C Squared Studios/Getty Images; 78 (top, left to right): © Steve Mason/Getty Images, © Ryan McVay/Getty Images, © Ingram Publishing/Alamy; 78 (middle, left to right): The McGraw-Hill Companies Inc./Ken Cavanagh Photographer, © Brand X Pictures/PunchStock, © image100/Alamy; 78 (bottom, left to right): © Siede Preis/Getty Images, © Prokopenko Alexander/ITAR-TASS/CORBIS, © Karl Weatherly/Getty Images; 80 (left): © Brand X Pictures/PunchStock; 80 (right); © Getty Images; 81 (both): © Creatas/PunchStock; 83 (left): © Ryan McVay/Getty Images; 83 (right): © BananaStock/PunchStock; 88 (top, left to right): © Royalty-Free/CORBIS, © Photodisc/Getty Images; 88 (middle, left to right): © Brand X Pictures/PunchStock, © Arthur S. Aubry/Getty Images; © Royalty-Free/CORBIS; 88 (bottom, left to right): © StockTrek/Getty Images, © PhotoDisc/Getty Images, © Creatas/PunchStock, © Digital Vision; 90 (top, left to right): © Image Source/PunchStock, © PhotoLink/Getty Images, © Thinkstock/Getty Images, © IT Stock/PunchStock; 90 (middle, left to right): © G.K. & Vikki Hart/Getty Images, © Golders/Alamy, © Brand X Pictures/PunchStock, © PhotoLink/Photodisc/Getty Images; 90 (bottom, left to right): © Brand X Pictures/PunchStock, © Getty Images, © Royalty-Free/CORBIS, © Creatas/PunchStock; 91 (top, left to right): © Brand X Pictures/PunchStock, © Getty Images, © Creatas/PunchStock, © Royalty-Free/CORBIS; 91 (Bottom, left to right): © USDA, © Stockdisc/PunchStock, © PhotoLink/Getty Images; © Creatas/PunchStock; 93: © Photodisc/PunchStock; 98 (top, left to right): © PhotoLink /Getty Images, © graficart.net/Alamy, © Dynamic Graphics Group /Creatas/Alamy; 98 (middle, left to right): © Creatas/PunchStock, © Ken Samuelsen/Getty Images, © Blend Images/Getty Images; 98 (bottom left): © Creatas/PunchStock; 100 (top to bottom): © Dynamic Graphics/JupiterImages, © Digital Vision/Getty Images, © PhotoDisc/Getty Images, © TRBfoto/Getty Images, © IndexStock/Alamy, © Royalty-Free/CORBIS; 101 (left to right): © BananaStock/JupiterImages, © Comstock Images/Alamy, © Judith Collins/Alamy; 103: © Ryan McVay/Getty Images; 111: © Paul Beard/Getty Images; 113: © Amos Morgan/Getty Images; 117: © PhotoLink/Getty Images; 128 (left to right): © PhotoLink/Getty Images, © Royalty-Free/CORBIS, © C Squared Studios/Getty Images, © Stockbyte Silver/Alamy; 133: © SW Productions/Getty Images.

We apologize for any apparent infringement of copyright and, if notified, the publisher will be pleased to rectify any errors or omissions at the earliest opportunity.